*A Slow Walk with
Early Christians*

A Slow Walk with Early Christians

90 Devotional Meditations on the Lives of Christians before AD 313

Edward B. Allen

Melbourne

A Slow Walk with Early Christians:
90 Devotional Meditations on the Lives of Christians before AD 313
by Edward B. Allen
Copyright © 2025 by Edward B. Allen
All rights reserved worldwide.
Reprinted with revisions 2026.

Published by Edward B. Allen
Melbourne, Florida
Email: edward.allen1949@gmail.com

ISBN: 979-8-9916936-2-2 (paperback)
979-8-9916936-3-9 (standard ebook *.epub)
979-8-9916936-4-6 (Kindle ebook)

Contact the publisher if you have questions regarding copying this book.

Scripture quotations marked CSB have been taken from the *Christian Standard Bible*® Copyright © 2017, 2020 by Holman Bible Publishers. Used by permission. *Christian Standard Bible*® and CSB ® are federally registered trademarks of Holman Bible Publishers.

Scriptures quoted in this work are noted by the following abbreviations.

> CSB, *Christian Standard Bible*, © 2017, 2020 Holman Bible Publishers
> KJV, *The Holy Bible, King James Version*, public domain

Cover design by Raney Day Creative, LLC. Cover image generated using Midjourney AI.

To Angie

Contents

Preface — xiii

Apostles, AD 30–100
1. A Lame Man 1
2. Saul of Tarsus 2
3. Saint Thaddeus 4
4. Ethiopian Eunuch 6
5. Saint Cornelius, the Centurion 7
6. Saint James, the Apostle 9
7. Saint Anianus, Bishop of Alexandria 10
8. Saint Thomas, the Apostle 11
9. Saint James, the Just 13
10. Persecution by Nero 15
11. Saints Processus and Martinian 16
12. Saint Torpes of Pisa 17
13. Saint Acestes 18

Contents

14	Saint Ursicinus of Ravenna	19
15	Flee from Jerusalem	20
16	Saint Anacletus, Bishop of Rome	21
17	Persecution by Domitian	22
18	Grandsons of Jude	24
19	Saint John, the Apostle	25

Defenders of the Faith, AD 100–200

20	Saint Ignatius, Bishop of Antioch	27
21	Saint Eudokia of Heliopolis	28
22	Persecution Reduced by Trajan	29
23	Saint Romulus	31
24	Saint Getulius	32
25	Saint Hyacinth of Caesarea	33
26	Saint Quadratus of Athens	34
27	Saint Justin Martyr	36
28	Saint Polycarp, Bishop of Smyrna	37
29	Saint Hermias of Comana	39
30	Saint Leucius, Bishop of Brindisi	40
31	Saint Abercius, Bishop of Hieropolis	42
32	Persecution in Gaul	43

Contents

33	Saint Irenaeus, Bishop of Lyon	44
34	Melitene Soldiers	45
35	Saint Pantaenus, the Philosopher	47
36	Saint Apollonius, the Apologist	48
37	Date of Easter	49

Persecution and Toleration, AD 200–303

38	Heretics who Relied on Logic	53
39	Saint Narcissus, Bishop of Jerusalem	55
40	Saint Alexander, Bishop of Jerusalem	56
41	Saint Callistus I, Bishop of Rome	57
42	Saints Theodore and Athenodore	59
43	Persecution by Maximinus, the Thracian	60
44	Saint Pontian, Bishop of Rome	61
45	Saint Gregory, the Wonderworker	62
46	Saint Fabian, Bishop of Rome	64
47	Saint Alexander, Bishop of Comana	65
48	Persecution by Decius	66
49	Saint Dionysius, Bishop of Alexandria	67

Contents

50	Saint Felix of Nola	69
51	Saints Abdon and Sennen	70
52	Saint Agatha of Sicily	71
53	Saint Christopher	73
54	Serapion, the Repentant	74
55	Persecution by Valerian	75
56	Saint Saturninus, Bishop of Toulouse	77
57	Exile of Saint Dionysius, Bishop of Alexandria	78
58	Saint Lawrence of Rome	80
59	Repentant from Heresy	81
60	Saint Fructuosus, Bishop of Tarragona	83
61	During the Plague	84
62	Saint Dionysius, Bishop of Rome	86
63	Saint Astyrius	87
64	Saint Marinus	88
65	Saint Anatolius of Laodicea, Syria	90
66	Saint Valentine of Rome	91
67	Saint Castulus	92
68	Saints Comas and Damian	93
69	Saint Sebastian	95

Contents

70 Saints Primus and Felician 96
71 Saints Cassian of Tangier and Genesius of Arles 98
72 Saint Andrew, the Tribune 99
73 Saint Fabius 101
74 Before the Great Persecution 102

The Great Persecution, AD 303–313

75 The Great Persecution by Diocletian 105
76 Soldiers 106
77 Saint George 107
78 Saint Genesius of Rome 109
79 Saint Felix, Bishop of Thibiuca 110
80 Saint Erasmus, Bishop of Formia 112
81 Saint Luxorius 113
82 Saint Pantaleon 114
83 Saint Phocas, the Gardener 115
84 Saints Felix and Adauctus 117
85 Saints Marcellinus and Peter 118
86 Beasts in the Arena 119
87 Saint Adrian of Nicomedia 121
88 Saint Peter, Bishop of Alexandria 122

xi

| 89 | The End of Persecution | 123 |
| 90 | Martyrs | 124 |

Index 127

About the author 133

Preface

Applying personal poetry like the Psalms to my life is easy, but history? Is the history of early Christians relevant to my spiritual walk in today's society? Even though our world today is quite different from the Roman empire, we face some of the same spiritual challenges they did.

Instead of evaluating historical evidence or analyzing the theology of early authors, this book draws spiritual applications from the lives of early Christians and related Scriptures.

This book is a collection of devotional meditations, slowly walking through stories about Christians who lived between Pentecost and AD 313. The Edict of Milan by Constantine in AD 313 ended persecution of Christians in the Roman empire.

Almost all the Christians featured in these meditations are honored as "Saints" by the Roman Catholic Church and the Eastern Orthodox Church. Bishops of Rome are honored as "Popes" by the Roman Catholic Church. Most details are based on tradition, rather than historical records. Their lives are inspiring, even if historicity is debated by scholars. Almost all dates of events are uncertain. I as-

Preface

sume Pentecost was in about AD 30.

All specific sources of stories are in the notes. A major source was *Church History* by Eusebius.[1] The complete edition of his *Church History* was published in about AD 324. References to paragraphs in *Church History* consist of his book and chapter numbers, for example, "III.5" means "Book III, chapter 5," irrespective of the translation.

Another major source was Catholic.org,[2] supplemented by Wikipedia, which is referenced by Catholic.org. All Web addresses were current on November 14, 2025.

Background on Acts in the New Testament is from a commentary by Richard Longenecker.[3] Background on the Roman empire is from Paul Maier's comments in his translation of *Church History*.

The *Christian Standard Bible* (CSB) is quoted as the primary translation of the Bible. It is a modern translation based on the latest evangelical scholarship. Clarifications of quotes are in [brackets]. Scripture references consist of book, chapter, verses, and version (if relevant), for example, "John 3:16 (CSB)."

All titles and Scripture references are indexed.

---

[1] Paul L. Maier, *Eusebius: The Church History* (Grand Rapids, Michigan: Kregel, 2007). This is a translation with commentary.

[2] https://www.catholic.org/saints/stindex.php and https://en.wikipedia.org/wiki/List_of_Catholic_saints.

[3] Richard Longenecker, "The Acts of the Apostles," *The Expositor's Bible Commentary*, Vol. 9 (Grand Rapids, Michigan: Zondervan, 1981).

Preface

A word or phrase referred to as a word is in *italics*. The term *believer* is used as a synonym for *Christian* for variety and to avoid implying those who are merely cultural Christian church-goers. Male pronouns are sometimes used to indicate a person of either gender.

I thank my many Facebook friends for their encouraging responses to my series of devotional meditations. I am also thankful for helpful suggestions by my local Word Weavers International critique group and for the support of my wife, Angie.

E.B.A.

Apostles, AD 30–100

1   A Lame Man

> [The lame man] jumped up and started to walk, and he entered the temple with [Peter and John]—walking, leaping, and praising God.
>
> Acts 3:8 (CSB)

A certain man who was lame sat by a gate of the temple in Jerusalem every day, so he could beg for alms. He had been lame from birth and was over forty years old.[4]

In about AD 31, the apostles Peter and John went to the temple as usual for the prayer service. They saw the lame man, and Peter said, "In the name of Jesus Christ of Nazareth, get up and walk!" Peter grabbed his hand and lifted him up. Instantly, his feet and ankles became strong. He went into the temple area walking, leaping, and praising God. The crowd in the temple recognized the man and were amazed.

---
[4] Acts 3:1–4:22.

Apostles, AD 30–100

Peter and John then began preaching to the crowd about Jesus, but they were promptly arrested by the temple police. The Jewish governing council (Sanhedrin) interrogated them the next day. The healed man stood with Peter and John during the trial. The authorities couldn't deny that a miracle had happened, and the people were still giving glory to God. All the council could do was threaten Peter and John.

The Scriptures don't say what happened to the formerly lame man afterward. I suppose he became a Christian.

After being lame all his life, he had no hope of living a normal life. The lame man experienced a miracle that proved Jesus is the Messiah. He was so overcome with joy his legs kept walking and leaping.

Even when my situation appears to be hopeless, God is not limited by my expectations. He arranges for connections with people, advances in technology, miracles, or whatever else I need.

> PRAYER: Lord, thank you for your grace that gives me hope and resolution to hopeless situations. I will share your hope with others. Amen.

2 Saul of Tarsus

> [The crowd] dragged [Stephen] out of the city and began to stone him. And the witnesses laid their garments at the feet of a young man named Saul...

Saul of Tarsus

> Saul agreed with putting him to death.
>
> On that day a severe persecution broke out against the church in Jerusalem, and all except the apostles were scattered throughout the land of Judea and Samaria.
>
> Acts 7:58; 8:1 (CSB)

Saul was a young Jewish man in his 20s, studying in Jerusalem under Gamaliel, the famous Pharisee rabbi. Saul was from the city of Tarsus in the province of Cilicia.[5]

In about AD 33, Stephen, the deacon, preached about Jesus and performed miracles in Jerusalem.[6] He was very successful debating Greek-speaking Jews. They hated him.

Stephen was arrested on false charges and tried by the Jewish governing council (Sanhedrin). During his trial, Stephen preached about Jesus. Saul may have heard Stephen, because Gamaliel, his mentor, was a member of the council.

At the climax of Stephen's sermon, the angry crowd dragged Stephen out of the city. Saul took care of the men's outer clothes while they stoned Stephen to death. Like everyone else, Saul approved of his death.

Saul was a devout Pharisee. He thought Christians were blaspheming and should be punished.

---

[5]Regarding Saul, see https://www.catholic.org/saints/saint.php?saint_id=91.

[6]Acts 6:8–8:1. Regarding Stephen, see https://www.catholic.org/saints/saint.php?saint_id=137.

Apostles, AD 30–100

He arrested Christians until he had an encounter with Jesus on the road to Damascus. He became a Christian himself. His Greek name was "Paul."

Like Saul and the Greek-speaking Jews, some people today are so committed to their religion or atheism that no reasoned debate and no sermon can persuade them. But a crisis in life can lead to a life-changing encounter with Jesus.

> PRAYER: Lord, let me reach friends in crisis with the truth of the gospel and your grace. Amen.

3 Saint Thaddeus

> Summoning his twelve disciples, [Jesus] gave them authority over unclean spirits, to drive them out and to heal every disease and sickness... "As you go, proclaim, 'The kingdom of heaven has come near.' "
>
> Matthew 10:1,7 (CSB)

Jesus' fame reached the frontier of the Roman Empire.[7] Governor Abgar[8] heard about the healings and miracles Jesus did, so he wrote a letter to Jesus asking him to come to Edessa, his capital, to heal him. Jesus declined but promised to send a disciple

---
[7] Eusebius, I.13 and II.1. According to tradition, https://www.catholic.org/saints/saint.php?saint_id=127. Thaddeus was martyred in about AD 66.

[8] Abgar's title was "toparch," similar to a governor.

Saint Thaddeus

later. After his resurrection and ascension, the Holy Spirit directed the Apostle Thomas in about AD 34 to send the disciple Thaddeus to Edessa to fulfill Jesus' promise.

After arriving in the pagan city, Thaddeus began healing people. Reports came to the governor, who sent for him. In the presence of the court officials, the governor verified that Thaddeus was the answer to his letter to Jesus and expressed his faith. So Thaddeus put his hand on the governor and he was instantly healed.

The next day Thaddeus preached to the entire city about Jesus and the way of salvation. As a result, the city was known as a Christian city for several hundred years.

Jesus gave his disciples authority to heal diseases and to preach the gospel. They have been doing so ever since. God has been faithful.

Like Thaddeus, I am a disciple. Like Thaddeus, I will go where the Holy Spirit sends me, perhaps just to the grocery store. The Lord knows if there is someone there who needs encouragement. Wherever I go, I get to share the gospel.

I may not get to speak with governors, presidents, or kings, but like Thaddeus, I can pray for ordinary people.

> PRAYER: Lord, I will go where you send me. According to the occasion, I'll encourage others and pray for the sick like Thaddeus did. Amen.

4 Ethiopian Eunuch

> So [Philip] got up and went [toward Gaza]. There was an Ethiopian man, a eunuch and high official of Candace, queen of the Ethiopians, who was in charge of her entire treasury. He had come to worship in Jerusalem and was sitting in his chariot on his way home, reading the prophet Isaiah aloud.
> Acts 8:27–28 (CSB)

In about AD 34, an Ethiopian eunuch, who was the treasurer of the queen of the Kingdom of Kush,[9] made a pilgrimage to Jerusalem to worship the God of the Jews. He obtained a scroll containing the prophecy of Isaiah, and read it aloud as he returned home in his chariot.

He noticed a Jewish man, Philip, the deacon,[10] running next to the chariot who asked if he understood what he was reading. The eunuch then invited Philip into his chariot.

Philip explained the gospel, beginning with how Isaiah 53:7 and other Old Testament Scriptures prophesied about Jesus. When they came to some water, the eunuch asked to be baptized. When he came up from the water, Philip disappeared. The eunuch continued home rejoicing in his newfound faith.

---

[9] The Kingdom of Kush was in modern Sudan and was called "Ethiopia" at that time.

[10] Acts 8:26–39. https://www.catholic.org/saints/saint.php?saint_id=776.

The eunuch was a royal official. He was not too proud to go all the way to Jerusalem to worship the most high god, the God of the Jews. He supposed that reading the prophet Isaiah would help him understand their religion. He was seeking true religion. When he met Philip, he found out that faith in Jesus was what he was looking for.

Many people today are seeking true religion. Religious ceremonies are not enough. Reading something incomprehensible is not enough. Simple faith in Jesus is what will satisfy.

> PRAYER: Lord, I want to communicate the gospel clearly to seekers, like Philip did. Amen.

5 Saint Cornelius, the Centurion

> There was a man in Caesarea named Cornelius, a centurion of what was called the Italian Regiment. He was a devout man and feared God along with his whole household. He did many charitable deeds for the Jewish people and always prayed to God.
> Acts 10:1–2 (CSB)

Cornelius was a centurion in the Roman army in an Italian unit.[11] He was stationed in Caesarea, Pales-

---

[11] Acts 10:1–48. According to tradition, https://www.catholic.org/saints/saint.php?saint_id=2745. Cornelius became the first bishop of Caesarea, Palestine.

tine. He was a devout man who was generous to the poor and prayed often to the God of the Jews.

In about AD 38, an angel appeared to him, telling him that God had received his prayers. The angel told him to send for a Jew named Simon Peter who was staying in the city of Joppa. So he sent two of his servants and a devout soldier to fetch Peter.

At that time, Jews avoided social contact with Gentiles. Peter had a vision teaching him not to call any person unclean based on race. As the men from Cornelius arrived at the gate of the house, the Holy Spirit told Peter to go with them without reservation. So Peter and some of the Jewish Christians from Joppa went with them to Caesarea.

Cornelius had received word they were coming, and had gathered his relatives and close friends to hear what Peter had to say. They were probably all Gentiles. As Peter was explaining the gospel, the Holy Spirit suddenly fell on all those listening, like what happened to the apostles on Pentecost. They spoke in other languages and praised God. Those from Joppa were amazed that God had given the Holy Spirit to Gentiles.

Peter responded by arranging for all of them to be baptized in water. Peter and the group from Joppa stayed with Cornelius for a few days.

Cornelius heard from God and obeyed. He didn't know what to expect. Cornelius and everyone else in the house were surprised by what happened. Their faith was stirred and they became Christians.

I have been surprised many times when I just did something simple the Holy Spirit nudged me to do. Sometimes someone's faith was stirred.

> PRAYER: Lord, I will act promptly when you nudge me to do something. Obeying you always has good results. Amen.

6 Saint James, the Apostle

> [Jesus said,] "But I tell you, love your enemies and pray for those who persecute you."
>
> Matthew 5:44 (CSB)

Herod Agrippa, king of Judea, arrested and executed James, the Apostle, in about AD 44.[12]

The man who led James to court was so moved by his testimony that the man declared he had become a Christian. He was promptly condemned. As he and James were being led away, he asked James for forgiveness. James replied, "Peace be with you," and they were beheaded together.

The Jewish leaders hated James. He may have assumed the man leading him to his trial was like them, an enemy. But James knew that as a follower of Jesus he must love his enemies. James had forgiven this man, and when he asked for forgiveness, James comforted him with a blessing.

---

[12] Acts 12:1–2. James, the Apostle, the son of Zebedee, was one of Jesus' twelve disciples. He was the brother of John, the Apostle. Eusebius II.9. According to tradition, https://www.catholic.org/saints/saint.php?saint_id=59.

Apostles, AD 30–100

Today, I could easily encounter someone who hates me. It could be a competitor in business, a rival at the office, or a fan of an opposing sports team. I must respond graciously, even when persecuted.

> PRAYER: Lord, it is hard to respond with love to those who hate me and persecute me. Help me to love my enemies. Amen.

7 Saint Anianus, Bishop of Alexandria

> [Jesus said to seventy disciples,] "Heal the sick who are there, and tell them, 'The kingdom of God has come near you.'"
>
> Luke 10:9 (CSB)

Mark, the Evangelist, went to Alexandria, Egypt, in about AD 49.[13] As he approached Alexandria, the strap of his sandal broke. He found a cobbler, named Anianus, to fix it.[14]

---

[13] Mark, the Evangelist, was the author of the Gospel of Mark and was a relative of Barnabas. According to tradition, https://www.catholic.org/saints/saint.php?saint_id=305. Mark was martyred in Alexandria in about AD 68.

[14] Regarding Anianus, according to tradition, see https://www.catholic.org/saints/saint.php?saint_id=1412. In about AD 62, Mark appointed Anianus as bishop of Alexandria. Anianus died in about AD 85. Anianus is honored as a Patriarch of Alexandria in the Eastern Orthodox and Coptic churches.

As Anianus was working on the sandal, his awl accidentally stabbed his hand. Taking advantage of the situation, Mark explained about Jesus and healed the wound.

Anianus took Mark home and his entire household was converted and baptized. This marked the beginning of the Christian community in Alexandria. Anianus became Mark's assistant.

The strap on Angie's sandal was about to break, so she found a cobbler, named Dave. As they talked, she found out his heart had a medical problem. She asked if he wanted prayer. With his approval, she prayed for healing out loud then and there.

I must be alert. When someone complains about a medical problem, I can respond like Mark and Angie did, with instant prayer. Most people are surprised and grateful.

> PRAYER: Lord, I will pray for healing whenever the occasion arises. I trust you for good results. Amen.

8 Saint Thomas, the Apostle

> [Jesus said,] "Go, therefore, and make disciples of all nations, baptizing them in the name of the Father and of the Son and of the Holy Spirit, teaching them to observe everything I have commanded

you. And remember, I am with you always, to the end of the age."
Matthew 28:19–20 (CSB)

In about AD 52, Thomas traveled to the Malabar coast of India (modern Kerala state).[15] He worked miracles and founded seven major churches and other smaller churches. He was martyred in about AD 72 in southeast India (modern Tamil Nadu state).

Today, those Christians whose heritage is from Thomas are called "Saint Thomas Christians."[16] Many families claim ancestors who were baptized by Thomas. In 2011, about 18% of Kerala's population were Christians. Of the Christians, about 71% were Saint Thomas Christians, members of multiple denominations. Over the centuries, the Saint Thomas Christians have adopted a variety of rites, affiliations, and denominations.

Thomas and his wife are Saint Thomas Christians living in America. My wife and I started a home Bible study with them. The group grew to five families from five countries, speaking five languages, and attending four local churches. Whenever we read the Scriptures aloud, we read in the native language of each family. Whenever we prayed for each other, we prayed aloud in our native languages. We were international disciples of

---

[15] According to tradition, https://www.catholic.org/saints/saint.php?saint_id=410.

[16] Regarding Saint Thomas Christians, see https://en.wikipedia.org/wiki/Saint_Thomas_Christians. Dates are according to the traditions of Saint Thomas Christians.

Jesus. The group met for a couple of years until members moved away.

Like Thomas, the Apostle, whenever I encounter someone from another country, I have the opportunity to put the Great Commission (above) into practice by making disciples and teaching the Bible.

> PRAYER: Lord, give me insight to share the gospel with internationals I meet. Amen.

9 Saint James, the Just

> James, a servant of God and of the Lord Jesus Christ: To the twelve tribes dispersed abroad. Greetings.
> James 1:1 (CSB)

James, the Just, was called a brother of Jesus (or a relative) and was an elder at the Council of Jerusalem in about AD 50.[17]

In about AD 62, Paul escaped the plot of the Jewish leaders and was sent to Rome.[18] Frustrated, they arrested James, who was the Bishop of Jerusalem.[19]

---

[17] James, the Just, was not one of Jesus' twelve disciples. He was the author of a letter in the New Testament. Regarding the Council of Jerusalem, see Acts 15:6–21.

[18] Regarding Paul's escape, see Acts 23:12–27:1.

[19] Eusebius, II.1 and II.23. According to tradition, https://www.catholic.org/saints/saint.php?saint_id=356.

James was highly respected in Jerusalem, so the Jewish leaders demanded that he convince the crowd at Passover that Jesus is not the Messiah. They forced him stand at the parapet on the roof of the temple. Then James testified about Jesus, the Messiah, to all the people. He preached that Jesus was raised from the dead, that he is now seated in heaven, and that he will come again in power.

The leaders were furious. They realized they had made a big mistake, so they threw him down from the roof. However, the fall did not kill him. As they were stoning him, James prayed for his persecutors. One of them hit him in the head with a club and killed him.

In the first verse of his letter (above), James acknowledged that Jesus is the Christ (the Messiah). James knew the Jewish leaders were trying to manipulate him to give the speech they wanted. He didn't say much until he spoke to the crowd.

Sometimes others will try to manipulate me to join them in worldly activities. This is similar to denying Jesus is the Messiah. Like James, I will resist the pressure and speak the truth of the gospel anyway.

> PRAYER: Lord, reveal when others are manipulating me, so I can speak the truth, irrespective of what others may think. Amen.

10 Persecution by Nero

> [Jesus said,] "You are blessed when they insult you and persecute you and falsely say every kind of evil against you because of me. Be glad and rejoice, because your reward is great in heaven. For that is how they persecuted the prophets who were before you."
>
> Matthew 5:11–12 (CSB)

There were Christians in Rome before Paul wrote his letter to the Romans in about AD 56. The Christians were accused of being "atheists," because they would not participate in civic festivals which included worshiping idols. Christians were an easy target in Roman society.

Nero was the first emperor to persecute the Christians.[20] When a fire devastated Rome in AD 64, the populace thought he was responsible. Shifting blame, he falsely accused the Christians of arson and decreed punishment, killing whomever he could find. The persecution was local, but both Paul and Peter, who were in Rome at the time, were martyred. Nero committed suicide in AD 68, and the persecution ended.

Jesus said I am blessed by God whenever I face false accusations and persecution, because reward in heaven is more valuable than any loss in this life.

> PRAYER: Lord, let me see persecution for your sake from an eternal perspec-

---
[20] Eusebius, II.25. Maier, p. 79.

tive. I want my life to bring you glory. Amen.

11 Saints Processus and Martinian

> Jesus stood up and cried out, "If anyone is thirsty, let him come to me and drink. The one who believes in me, as the Scripture has said, will have streams of living water flow from deep within him." He said this about the Spirit.
> John 7:37–39 (CSB)

Processus and Martinian were wardens where the apostles Peter and Paul were imprisoned in Rome.[21] After a spring miraculously flowed inside the prison, they became Christians and were baptized in the prison waters. When the Emperor Nero found out, they were arrested, tortured, and beheaded in about AD 65.

Seeing a miraculous spring inside their prison probably convinced these jailers to worship the God of the Christians. When they believed, they found out that the Holy Spirit in them was like that spring, "living water."

When I became a believer, I discovered that the Holy Spirit communicated with me like a spring of water. He "spoke" in Scriptures, sermons, books,

---

[21] According to tradition, https://www.catholic.org/saints/saint.php?saint_id=5485.

nudges, and so on. He internally whispered to my soul, "This is for you," or "Go this way."

> PRAYER: Lord, thank you for the Holy Spirit, my source of "living water." Amen.

12 Saint Torpes of Pisa

> [Jesus said,] "Everyone who will acknowledge me before others, I will also acknowledge him before my Father in heaven. But whoever denies me before others, I will also deny him before my Father in heaven."
> Matthew 10:32–33 (CSB)

Torpes was a native of Pisa, Italy, and was a member of the Emperor Nero's bodyguard.[22] He was converted by Paul, the Apostle.

When Nero celebrated the pagan goddess Diana in about AD 65, Torpes confessed being a Christian. As a loyal bodyguard, Torpes was expected to participate in the emperor's pagan ceremony. So he had to explain why he would not worship the idol. The emperor tried to persuade him to deny his faith. He would not, so Nero had him beheaded.

---

[22] According to tradition, https://www.catholic.org/saints/saint.php?saint_id=2358.

Even though Torpes had a close relationship with the emperor, his relationship with Jesus was more important.

Like Nero, the people at my office sometimes implied worship of the company was required of all loyal employees. I had to explain that Jesus is more important.

> PRAYER: Lord, you are the most important thing in my life. Help me give a clear explanation when asked. Amen.

13 Saint Acestes

> For I [Paul] am already being poured out as a drink offering, and the time for my departure is close. I have fought the good fight, I have finished the race, I have kept the faith. There is reserved for me the crown of righteousness, which the Lord, the righteous Judge, will give me on that day, and not only to me, but to all those who have loved his appearing.
>
> 2 Timothy 4:6–8 (CSB)

Paul arrived at Rome as a prisoner.[23] After two years under house arrest, he was released, traveled to Spain, and returned to Rome. Paul was arrested and the Emperor Nero ordered his execution

---
[23] Acts 28:16,30–31.

Saint Ursicinus of Ravenna

in about AD 67. Paul wrote letters while imprisoned. He knew his death would be soon. In his second letter to Timothy (above), he expressed his confidence in Christ.

Acestes and two fellow Roman soldiers escorted Paul to his death.[24] After seeing Paul beheaded, the three soldiers declared their faith in Christ to those there and were promptly beheaded, too.

Acestes saw Paul was willing to die for Christ and had assurance of eternal life. Like Paul, Acestes has a crown of righteousness reserved for him.

An ungodly crowd can be intimidating. Even a friend's criticism can stir up fear. Taking a stand for what is right might be dangerous. But I have assurance of eternal life like Paul and Acestes.

> PRAYER: Lord, whenever standing for you is difficult, remind me about what you have reserved for me. Amen.

14 Saint Ursicinus of Ravenna

> Let us hold on to the confession of our hope without wavering, since he who promised is faithful.
>
> Hebrews 10:23 (CSB)

Ursicinus was a physician in the city of Ravenna,

---

[24]Eusebius, II.22. According to tradition, https://www.catholic.org/saints/saint.php?saint_id=1097.

Italy.[25] A physician is accustomed to helping others. His Christian faith motivated him even more to help the sick.

In spite of his good reputation, he was arrested and condemned to death for being a Christian during the persecution by the Emperor Nero. When his faith wavered, he was strengthened by another Christian's encouragement. He remembered that God is faithful to fulfill his promises. He had steadfast faith when he was martyred in about AD 67.

My faith may not be challenged like his was, but I am encouraged by the testimony of fellow believers. When I encounter believers whose faith is wavering, I will remind them of God's faithfulness.

> PRAYER: Lord, show me when someone needs encouragement in their faith, so I can share about your promises. Amen.

15 Flee from Jerusalem

> [Jesus said,] "So when you see the abomination of desolation, spoken of by the prophet Daniel, standing in the holy place (let the reader understand), then those in Judea must flee to the mountains."
>
> Matthew 24:15–16 (CSB)

Beginning in about AD 66, the Jews revolted against Roman rule (the First Jewish-Roman War). The

---

[25] According to tradition, https://www.catholic.org/saints/saint.php?saint_id=1891.

Roman general Vespasian invaded Palestine to put down the rebellion.

War was everywhere. The city of Jerusalem was chaotic. Jewish factions were fighting each other for control. In about AD 68, a prophetic oracle told the Christians in Jerusalem to leave the city.[26] They remembered the words of Jesus (above). They all went to the small town of Pella in the region of Perea, on the east side of the Jordan River.

By AD 69, the rebels had taken refuge in Jerusalem and closed the gates. Vespasian's son Titus besieged Jerusalem, which fell in AD 70.

In the middle of the confusion in Jerusalem, the Christians had to rely on the Lord. In my confusing situations, I will remember that following the direction of the Holy Spirit leads to peace.

> PRAYER: Lord, I will go when and where the Holy Spirit directs. Amen.

16 Saint Anacletus, Bishop of Rome

> And [the Lord] himself gave some to be apostles, some prophets, some evangelists, some pastors and teachers, to equip the saints for the work of ministry, to build up the body of Christ.
>
> Ephesians 4:11–12 (CSB)

---

[26] Eusebius, III.5. According to tradition of Saint Simon, Bishop of Jerusalem, https://www.catholic.org/saints/saint.php?saint_id=747.

Apostles, AD 30–100

After the persecution by Nero ended in AD 68, the Christian community in Rome grew so large that one bishop could not function as a pastor and teacher to everyone. While Anacletus was bishop, he established about twenty-five parishes in Rome and appointed leaders.[27]

The Lord equips people with various leadership gifts so that believers become mature and do good works. Anacletus had to discern those gifts to find good leaders for the parishes. Guidance by the Holy Spirit is necessary to find the best leaders.

A home Bible study my wife and I were leading became too large for the host home. We had to divide the group into two new groups with new leaders and new host homes. It was a difficult transition, because one of the new leaders resigned just before his group started. I suppose Anacletus faced similar issues.

> PRAYER: Lord, thank you for the guidance of the Holy Spirit when finding new leaders for believers. Amen.

17 Persecution by Domitian

> [Jesus said,] "Blessed are those who are persecuted because of righteousness, for the kingdom of heaven is theirs."
> Matthew 5:10 (CSB)

---

[27] According to tradition, https://www.catholic.org/saints/saint.php?saint_id=827. Anacetus was bishop of Rome from about AD 79 to 92.

Persecution by Domitian

The Emperor Domitian began persecuting the Christians in about AD 95.[28] Apparently, his edict was empire-wide. John, the Apostle, who was living in Ephesus in the province of Asia, was banished to the island of Patmos.[29] While John was there, he received an important vision from God. Domitian was assassinated in AD 96. The empire-wide persecution ended, and John returned to Ephesus.

By AD 95, John was an elderly man. He may have thought exile to Patmos meant the end of his ministry. However, God used the isolation of Patmos to reveal the last book of the Bible. Banishment that the world meant for harm resulted in a spiritual blessing for generations of believers, the book of Revelation.

I wonder if the busyness of Ephesus would have interfered with receiving the vision. For John, the interruption of his ministry was just temporary, because he resumed his work in Ephesus.

Sometimes I think I know how I can best serve the Lord. Then a disappointing twist in my circumstances comes along. The Lord then opens a different way to serve him that I never imagined.

> PRAYER: Lord, give me your perspective when circumstances interrupt my plans for serving you. I know spiritual fruit can come in surprising ways. Amen.

---

[28] Eusebius, III.17,18.
[29] Revelation 1:9.

Apostles, AD 30–100

18 Grandsons of Jude

> [Jesus said to the disciples,] "So when they arrest you and hand you over, don't worry beforehand what you will say, but say whatever is given to you at that time, for it isn't you speaking, but the Holy Spirit."
>
> Mark 13:11 (CSB)

In about AD 96, the Emperor Domitian ordered the execution of all descendants of the Jewish King David.[30] He had heard about the coming of Christ. I suppose he was paranoid about threats to his reign.

Two grandsons of Jude were arrested and brought before the emperor. Their grandfather wrote a letter in the New Testament.

They were asked if they were descended from King David, which they admitted. Their grandfather was a brother (or relative) of Jesus.

The emperor asked about their wealth. They said they only had the land they farmed. They proved that they were farmers by calluses on their hands.

The emperor asked about Christ and his kingdom. They explained that the kingdom of God is not of this world, but heavenly, and Jesus will return at the end of the world to judge everyone.

The emperor despised them. He thought they were simple folk, so he let them go free.

I may not be grilled by an emperor, but I may need to explain my faith. The Holy Spirit will give

---

[30] Eusebius, III.19,20. According to tradition.

me the words to say which will fit the occasion.

> PRAYER: Lord, thank you for helping me explain the gospel to those who don't know it or to those who misunderstand it. Amen.

19 Saint John, the Apostle

> My brothers and sisters, if any among you strays from the truth, and someone turns him back, let that person know that whoever turns a sinner from the error of his way will save his soul from death and cover a multitude of sins.
> James 5:19–20 (CSB)

After the persecution by the Emperor Domitian ended in about AD 96, John returned to Ephesus and traveled about the province of Asia, teaching the churches. By this time, John was an elderly man.[31]

While visiting a certain city, John committed a young man to the care of the local bishop.[32] The

---
[31] John, the Apostle, son of Zebedee, was one of Jesus' twelve disciples, and he was the brother of James, the Apostle. He was the author of the Gospel of John, three letters, and the book of Revelation in the New Testament. John died in about AD 100.

[32] Eusebius, III.23. Eusebius quoted a document by Clement I, Bishop of Rome, https://www.catholic.org/saints/saint.php?saint_id=228.

Apostles, AD 30–100

bishop converted and baptized the young man. However, the young man was corrupted by his friends and became the leader of a gang of bandits.

When John returned to that city, he found out what had become of the young man. He quickly went with a guide to the bandits' mountain camp. He told the guard at the gate, "Take me to your leader!"

When the young man saw John coming, he began to run away. Elderly John ran after him, shouting. The young man stopped, looked at the ground, and began weeping. He threw his arms around John, pleading for forgiveness.

John assured him that he had forgiveness from the Savior. He led the young man back to the city and did not leave until through prayer, fasting, and instruction the young man was restored to the church.

This story illustrates persistence, repentance, and reconciliation. No matter how low someone has fallen, God's forgiveness is available.

> PRAYER: Lord, I will be persistent in reaching out with your mercy to those who have fallen. Amen.

Defenders of the Faith, AD 100-200

20 Saint Ignatius, Bishop of Antioch

> No foul language should come from your mouth, but only what is good for building up someone in need, so that it gives grace to those who hear.
>
> Ephesians 4:29 (CSB)

Ignatius was the bishop of Antioch in the Roman province of Syria.[33] In about AD 107, he was arrested and condemned to death for his faith in Christ. He was sent from Antioch to Rome for execution.

Elderly Ignatius and the soldiers guarding him traveled by land. As they passed through each city,

---

[33]Eusesbius III.36. According to tradition, https://www.catholic.org/saints/saint.php?saint_id=677. The letters by Ignatius have survived to today.

Ignatius encouraged the Christians there. During the trip, he wrote letters to the churches in seven cities. The letters conveyed encouragement, inspiration, the apostles' teaching, and right practice for believers. He expressed his faith while facing death.

When they reached Rome, he was killed by lions in an arena for a pagan crowd.

I've written letters to friends and family most of my life, such as a newsy letter at Christmas time. Technology has made communicating easier and faster. Email is now my standard. Long distance telephone calls are no longer expensive. Text messages and social media make short messages easy. Christian content is naturally part of my letters, because it is part of my life.

> PRAYER: Lord, let my letters build up the faith of others, like those of Ignatius. Amen.

21 Saint Eudokia of Heliopolis

> Through [Jesus] let us continually offer up to God a sacrifice of praise, that is, the fruit of lips that confess his name. Don't neglect to do what is good and to share, for God is pleased with such sacrifices.
> Hebrews 13:15–16 (CSB)

Eudokia was a native of the city of Heliopolis in the Roman province of Phoenicia.[34] As a pagan, she led a sinful life with many lovers.

One night, she was awakened by singing in the house of a Christian woman next door. She also could hear the preaching of a visiting elder. Her heart was grieved because of her sinful lifestyle.

The next day she contacted the elder. After listening to his teaching, she was converted and filled with joy and love for Christ. To demonstrate her repentance, she gave away her wealth and forsook her previous life.

I never know who is listening when I sing or talk about Jesus. I might be playing guitar and singing in a park or on the porch. I might be talking about Jesus in a restaurant or at home with the windows open. Somebody who needs Jesus may be listening.

> PRAYER: Lord, guide my songs and conversations. I will keep praising you and speaking about you, because I have no idea who will hear it. Amen.

22 Persecution Reduced by Trajan

> Conduct yourselves honorably among the Gentiles, so that when they slander you as evildoers, they will observe your

---

[34] According to tradition, https://www.oca.org/saints/lives/2010/03/01/100625-martyr-eudokia-of-heliopolis. Eudokia was martyred in about AD 107.

good works and will glorify God on the day he visits.

1 Peter 2:12 (CSB)

After the death of the Emperor Domitian in AD 96, Christians continued to be persecuted in various places by the pagan populace and local officials.

In about AD 112, Pliny, the Younger, was governor of the Roman region of Bythinia. As the judge in death-sentence cases, he was surprised that so many Christians were being prosecuted before him. So he wrote to the Emperor Trajan for guidance. A summary of Pliny's letter says,[35]

> [Pliny] found nothing wicked in their behavior, other than their unwillingness to worship idols. He further informed [the Emperor Trajan] that the Christians rose at dawn, sang hymns to Christ as a god, and upheld their teachings by forbidding murder, adultery, fraud, robbery, and the like.

In response, Trajan issued an edict that Christians were no longer to be hunted, but should be prosecuted if identified. This reduced the threat to the Christians.

Peter instructed believers to live honestly in daily life, so that worldly people will see their good works (above). Worldly authorities, like Governor Pliny, may recognize the good works. But even

---

[35]Eusebius, III.33. Eusebius quoted Tertullian, who was an early Christian author.

Saint Romulus

if they criticize and slander, they will glorify God when Jesus returns.

> PRAYER: Lord, let me consistently live honorably among the worldly people around me. I can see the emptiness of their criticism and slander. Amen.

23 Saint Romulus

> Your throne, God,
> is forever and ever,
> and the scepter of your kingdom
> is a scepter of justice.
>
> Hebrews 1:8 (CSB)

Romulus was a member of the imperial court of the Emperor Trajan.[36] He saw Christians being persecuted, tortured, and condemned. In about AD 112, he spoke out against the injustice.

Even though Romulus had an influential position, the emperor was offended and commanded that Romulus be arrested, tortured, and executed in the same manner as those he defended.

Romulus recognized the injustices of his times. Deception in the media, corruption of officials, and bias in the courts seem rampant today. I am praying for truth, righteousness, and justice in our land, because justice is a foundation of the kingdom of God.

---

[36] According to tradition, https://www.catholic.org/saints/saint.php?saint_id=4637.

While showing respect for those in authority, I will pray, and like Romulus, I will press for justice in my circle of influence. Those in authority may accept or reject my pleas, but I must be persistent.

> PRAYER: Lord, use my influence to speak clearly for justice. Show me the best way to help victims of injustice. Amen.

24 Saint Getulius

> But as for you, exercise self-control in everything, endure hardship, do the work of an evangelist, fulfill your ministry.
> 2 Timothy 4:5 (CSB)

Getulius was a Roman army officer. When he became a Christian, he resigned his commission and retired to his estate near Tivoli, Italy. His family and his brother Amantius also became Christians.[37]

Caerealis, an imperial official, was sent to arrest him, but Getulius converted him. Then another officer, named Primitivus, was sent to arrest him, but Getulius also converted him.

In about AD 120, Getulius, his brother, and the two officials he converted were tortured and martyred together at Tivoli.

---

[37] According to tradition, https://www.catholic.org/saints/saint.php?saint_id=873.

I don't know what Getulius told the two officials that convinced them to become Christians, but Getulius did the work of an evangelist. The Holy Spirit had prepared them to hear about Jesus and our hope in Christ.

I consider the worldly people I encounter to be appointments God has prepared for me. They may not be Roman officials, but like Getulius, I can share the gospel with them.

> PRAYER: Lord, help me do the work of an evangelist for the people you send me. Amen.

25 Saint Hyacinth of Caesarea

> [From the apostles and the elders, your brothers:] For it was the Holy Spirit's decision—and ours—not to place further burdens on you beyond these requirements: that you abstain from food offered to idols, ... You will do well if you keep yourselves from these things.
> Acts 15:28–29 (CSB)

Hyacinth was from Caesarea in the Roman province of Cappadocia. He was raised by Christian parents. As a young boy, he became an assistant to the chamberlain of the Emperor Trajan. This job took him to Rome.[38]

He was accused of being a Christian when others in the household noticed he did not participate in the usual sacrifices to the pagan gods. He had to decide whether to identify with his peers or to identify as a Christian.

He admitted he was a Christian, so he was imprisoned and tortured. The jailers deliberately fed him only meat offered to idols.[39] At every mealtime, would he identify as an ordinary Roman or as a Christian? He refused the meat offered to idols and starved to death in about AD 120. Hyacinth was twelve years old.

Every boy or girl, especially those raised by Christian parents, must decide for themselves. Will they yield to peer pressure or identify as a Christian? When they get older, will they act like their worldly friends?

> PRAYER: Lord, I intercede for the young people I know that they decide for themselves to follow you. Amen.

26   Saint Quadratus of Athens

> [Be] ready at any time to give a defense to anyone who asks you for a reason for

---

[38] According to tradition, https://www.catholic.org/saints/saint.php?saint_id=3828.

[39] Acts 15:6–29. The Jerusalem Council was held in about AD 50.

Saint Quadratus of Athens

> the hope that is in you.
> 1 Peter 3:15 (CSB)

Quadratus was a student of the apostles and settled in Athens as an independent teacher. He faced criticism for his faith in this city full of philosophers.

In about AD 124, the Emperor Hadrian visited Athens. Quadratus presented a document to him defending the validity of Christianity.[40]

The document by Quadratus is one the earliest to defend the faith. He was intellectually rigorous and upheld the apostles' teaching. He argued that the miracles of Jesus were never challenged, because those who were healed were living in Palestine for many years. The miracles and the testimony of witnesses were evidence for the validity of the gospel.

Today, atheists criticize Christianity with detailed arguments. Books that defend the faith with intellectual rigor help prepare ordinary believers to counter the arguments of atheists. Sometimes such a book convinces an atheist to become a Christian.

> PRAYER: Lord, organize my thoughts with reasons for the hope I have in you. Amen.

---

[40]Eusebius, IV.3. According to tradition, https://www.catholic.org/saints/saint.php?saint_id=4678. Copies of his document were widely circulated among the churches. He was martyred in about AD 129.

27 Saint Justin Martyr

> Be careful that no one takes you captive through philosophy and empty deceit based on human tradition, based on the elements of the world, rather than Christ.
>
> Colossians 2:8 (CSB)

Justin was a Gentile from the city of Flavia Neapolis in Samaria, Palestine.[41]

After studying various kinds of Greek philosophy he became an ardent follower of Plato. While he was a Platonic philosopher, he noticed that Christians were unafraid to die for their faith. He reasoned that they could not be wicked people, because it would be illogical for the wicked to give up their lifestyle.

One day as he walked near the seashore, he had a long philosophical conversation with an old man. The old man argued that the testimonies of prophets were more reliable than the reasoning of philosophers.

Pondering the old man's reasoning and the testimony of the martyrs, Justin became a Christian in about AD 130. He adopted the clothing style of a philosopher and traveled about, teaching the gospel as the only true philosophy.

He settled in Rome and established a school. He was a prolific writer and several of his documents

---

[41] Eusebius, IV.8,12,16,18. https://www.catholic.org/saints/saint.php?saint_id=4144. Justin was beheaded for the faith in about AD 165. He is now known as Justin Martyr.

have survived to today, including defenses of the faith addressed to the Emperor Antoninus Pius and to his successor, the Emperor Marcus Aurelius.

Justin was an intellectual who knew traditional philosophy very well. He also was not deceived by the elements of this world.

Sometimes I encounter intellectuals who like to discuss philosophy. Justin's writings show how the gospel is more reasonable and more reliable than what worldly philosophers have to say.

> PRAYER: Lord, reveal the deceit of the world's reasoning. Amen.

28 Saint Polycarp, Bishop of Smyrna

> Pursue righteousness, godliness, faith, love, endurance, and gentleness. Fight the good fight of the faith. Take hold of eternal life to which you were called and about which you have made a good confession in the presence of many witnesses.
> 1 Timothy 6:11–12 (CSB)

Polycarp was converted by John, the Apostle, heard his teaching, and was appointed bishop of the city of Smyrna in the province of Asia.[42]

---

[42] Eusebius, III.36; IV.15, which quotes the *Martyrdom of Polycarp*. According to tradition, https://www.catholic.org/saints/saint.php?saint_id=5532.

Defenders of the Faith, AD 100–200

Persecution of the Christians flared in the province of Asia in about AD 156. By this time, Polycarp was an elderly man, the beloved leader of the Christian community. After numerous Christians were martyred in the arena at Smyrna, the rabid pagan crowd called for Polycarp.

Friends persuaded Polycarp to leave the city for nearby farms. When the authorities tracked him down in the middle of the night, he welcomed them and fed them. On the way to the arena, the officer tried to persuade Polycarp to sacrifice to Caesar. In the arena, the governor offered to set him free if he would deny Christ, but Polycarp declared his loyalty to Jesus.

Frustrated, the governor threatened, "I have wild beasts. I'll throw you to them if you don't change your mind!"

Polycarp replied, "Call them."

The governor countered, "If you disregard the beasts, I'll have you consumed by fire unless you repent!"

Polycarp answered, "You threaten with a fire that burns for a time and is quickly extinguished. Yet a fire you know nothing about awaits the wicked in judgment to come and in eternal punishment."

The governor pronounced his sentence, and the angry crowd quickly brought wood and kindling. Polycarp calmly stood among the wood and prayed. The fire was lit. He died in the flames.

Ever since he was a young convert, Polycarp had followed Paul's charge to Timothy (above). He had led a life of "righteousness, godliness, faith, love, endurance, and gentleness." In the arena, he made a powerful confession of his loyalty to Christ, standing before the whole city.

Paul's charge to Timothy is also addressed to me. I must have the same qualities in my life as Polycarp, and I will confess my loyalty to Christ to anyone who will listen.

> PRAYER: Lord, let me show gentleness and boldness in the face of opposition. Amen.

29 Saint Hermias of Comana

> [Jesus said to the disciples,] "Go into all the world and preach the gospel to all creation… And these signs will accompany those who believe: …if they should drink anything deadly, it will not harm them;…"
>
> Mark 16:15–18 (CSB)

Hermias retired from the Roman army after a long career.[43] Upon discharge in about AD 160, he refused his pay and confessed his faith in Christ.

He was arrested and tried by the governor[44] in the city of Comana in the province of Cappadocia.

---

[43] According to tradition, https://www.catholic.org/saints/saint.php?saint_id=3743.

[44] A proconsul had similar duties as a governor.

Defenders of the Faith, AD 100–200

Hermias refused to deny Christ, and so he was condemned. He was tortured and thrown into a furnace. After three days he emerged from the furnace unhurt. So the frustrated governor called on a sorcerer. When the sorcerer saw Hermias drink two poisons without harm, the sorcerer admitted that Christ was more powerful. The sorcerer was promptly beheaded.

Throughout the tortures, Hermias gave thanks to Christ. Eventually, he was executed by the sword.

Hermias spread the gospel by his firm confession. Being miraculously saved from death by fire and by poison resulted in the salvation of the sorcerer. His thanksgiving and worship during all his tortures glorified God, culminating in his martyrdom.

> PRAYER: Lord, let me spread the gospel like Hermias. I will glorify you with a thankful heart. Amen.

30 Saint Leucius, Bishop of Brindisi

[In Iconium, Paul and Barnabus] stayed there a long time and spoke boldly for the Lord, who testified to the message of his grace by enabling them to do signs and wonders.

Acts 14:3 (CSB)

Saint Leucius, Bishop of Brindisi

Leucius was a missionary from Alexandria, Egypt, to the city of Brindisi, Italy, in the region of Apulia.[45] At that time, Brindisi was a major seaport and a pagan city.

When he arrived, Leucius preached in the surrounding region of Apulia during a drought. He claimed if the people would believe the gospel, then the rains would come. When the rains fell, the pagans were immediately converted. Shortly after this, Leucius became the bishop of the city of Brindisi in about AD 165.

In an agricultural society, a drought threatens everyone's welfare. When this Christian preacher miraculously made it rain, the people were receptive to the gospel. Miracle-working power was very persuasive. Miracles validated Leucius' preaching. Similarly, Paul and Barnabus saw miracles validate their message in Iconium.

The same is true today. Revivals in modern times have been marked by healings and other miracles. I've seen people experience a personal touch from God when they feel or witness God's power.

> PRAYER: Lord, bring revival to our land and demonstrate your supernatural power. Amen.

---

[45] According to tradition, https://www.catholic.org/saints/saint.php?saint_id=4267. Leucius was martyred in about AD 180.

31 Saint Abercius, Bishop of Hieropolis

[Jesus said to the disciples,] "Go into all the world and preach the gospel to all creation... And these signs will accompany those who believe: In my name they will drive out demons..."

Mark 16:15–17 (CSB)

Abercius was bishop of Hieropolis in the region of Phrygia Salutaris. When he was an elderly man, he visited Rome.[46]

While there, he was arrested and imprisoned. During his trial, the Emperor Marcus Aurelius demanded Abercius free his daughter from a demon. So he did. Abercius died in about AD 167.

Western civilization today denies demons exist, so casting them out is unusual. In the 1990s, an associate pastor of my church frequently set people free who came to his office for help. He exercised spiritual discernment to distinguish the effects of sin, medical issues, and demonic influence. When appropriate, he cast out demons.

> PRAYER: Lord, thank you for spiritual discernment, and your power over demons. Amen.

---

[46] According to tradition, https://www.catholic.org/saints/saint.php?saint_id=1074. Further details about Abercius' life are uncertain.

32 Persecution in Gaul

> [Jesus said,] "I have told you these things to keep you from stumbling. They will ban you from the synagogues. In fact, a time is coming when anyone who kills you will think he is offering service to God."
>
> John 16:1–2 (CSB)

In about AD 177, during the reign of the Emperor Marcus Aurelius, persecution of Christians flared in various places across the Roman empire. In the Roman culture, civic events and festivals routinely included worship of the pagan gods (idols). Everyone was expected to participate. However, Christians would not worship idols. This was highly offensive to the pagans.

In the province of Gaul, pagan mobs attacked Christians, especially in the cities of Vienne and Lyon.[47] They seized Christians, falsely accused them, abused them, and indicted them before city authorities. The Christians were imprisoned until the governor came to town for a trial. The governor, in turn, was furious at their refusal to worship the idols. When questioned, the Christians simply answered, "I am a Christian." The mobs and the governor thought they were honoring their gods by punishing the Christian "atheists."

Some Christians were so overcome by fear of death that they denied the Lord, worshiped an idol,

---

[47] Eusebius, V.1. Eusebius quotes a letter from the church in Gaul.

Defenders of the Faith, AD 100–200

and were released. Some later repented and joined the martyrs. Others were steadfast and endured horrible torture. Some died from the torture, and some were martyred in an arena.

Standing for what is right can be offensive to a worldly mob today. They may falsely accuse believers. They may sue in court to silence the gospel. Homeowner associations may penalize the innocent. Legislators may pass laws making righteousness a crime. The mob will think punishing believers means justice is served. Our times are similar to what the Christians in Gaul faced.

> PRAYER: Lord, when tumultuous times come, give me your peace. Amen.

33 Saint Irenaeus, Bishop of Lyon

> Dear friends, do not believe every spirit, but test the spirits to see if they are from God, because many false prophets have gone out into the world.
>
> 1 John 4:1 (CSB)

Irenaeus was a priest in the city of Lyon in the province of Gaul.[48] In about AD 177, he was the courier of a letter to the bishop of Rome. While

---

[48] According to tradition, https://www.catholic.org/saints/saint.php?saint_id=291. Irenaeus died in about AD 202. Complete translations of *Against Heresies* from Greek into Latin have survived to today.

he was gone, severe persecution of the Christians arose in Lyon, and Pothinus, Bishop of Lyon, was martyred with many others. Irenaeus returned to the city after the persecution had subsided and became the new bishop.

In a few years, the heresy of Gnosticism started to affect his flock. Gnostics taught that special secret knowledge was necessary for salvation.

In response, Irenaeus wrote a treatise, *Against Heresies*, which systematically exposed the fallacies of Gnosticism and other heresies. He clearly contrasted them with the apostles' teaching and Old Testament Scriptures. Copies of his treatise were widely circulated throughout the empire, and Gnosticism was no longer a threat to the faith.

Heresies like Gnosticism have arisen from time to time over the centuries. Even today there are sects that claim some prophet's special revelation is necessary. John's first letter warned us about false prophets (above). Irenaeus set the standard for correct teaching from the whole Bible.

> PRAYER: Lord, I need your help to recognize when a sect is twisting the Scriptures. Amen.

34 Melitene Soldiers

> The prayer of a righteous person is very powerful in its effect. Elijah was a human being as we are, and he prayed earnestly that it would not rain, and for

Defenders of the Faith, AD 100–200

> three years and six months it did not rain on the land. Then he prayed again, and the sky gave rain and the land produced its fruit.
>
> James 5:16–18 (CSB)

In about AD 177, the Emperor Marcus Aurelius fought German tribes and their allies, the Sarmatians.[49]

The entire Roman army could hardly fight, because they had run out of water and were very thirsty. The soldiers in the Melitene Legion were from Cappadocia and were mostly Christians, so they all prayed, kneeling on the ground.

The enemy soldiers were surprised to see Romans kneeling on the ground. Both sides were amazed when lightning fell on the enemy and drove them away, while refreshing rain fell on the Roman army.

The Melitene soldiers knew their prayers asking for rain were just as powerful as Elijah's, the famous prophet of the Old Testament. James explained (above) that we are like Elijah. Just like the prayers of the Melitene soldiers, God pays attention to believers' prayers today.

> PRAYER: Lord, thank you for answering my prayers, even if I ask for rain. Amen.

---

[49]Eusebius, V.5. According to tradition. This battle may have been near the border of the empire at the Danube River.

35 Saint Pantaenus, the Philosopher

> Be diligent to present yourself to God as one approved, a worker who doesn't need to be ashamed, correctly teaching the word of truth.
>
> 2 Timothy 2:15 (CSB)

Pantaenus was a famous Stoic philosopher who led a Christian school in Alexandria, Egypt, from about AD 180.[50]

Stoicism was a ancient pagan Greek philosophy that was well-respected in the Roman world. After Pantaenus became a Christian, he sought to reconcile his new faith with the intellectual ideas of his day.

Although none of his writings have survived to today, we know he wrote about interpreting the Bible, the Trinity, the importance of Christ, and opposing the heresy of Gnosticism. He prepared students to defend the Christian faith.

Pantaenus believed education of Christians was important. Today, there are many Christian schools at all levels of education. Like other churches, in the 1990s, my church started a Christian school for young children, and then gradually added grades up through twelfth grade. The church also hosted a college-level correspondence Bible school for international students. Such schools teach the Bible and

---

[50] According to tradition, https://www.catholic.org/saints/saint.php?saint_id=808. Pantaenus died about AD 200.

prepare students for life based on Christian principles.

Less formal Christian education is also common, such as Sunday Schools and home Bible studies. These are where I have learned about godly living.

> PRAYER: Lord, thank you for Christian schools and for the home Bible studies where I have learned so much. Amen.

36 Saint Apollonius, the Apologist

> For where there is envy and selfish ambition, there is disorder and every evil practice. But the wisdom from above is first pure, then peace-loving, gentle, compliant, full of mercy and good fruits, unwavering, without pretense. And the fruit of righteousness is sown in peace by those who cultivate peace.
> James 3:16–18 (CSB)

Apollonius was a well-respected Roman senator who was a Christian.[51] He was denounced for being a Christian, and then was arrested and tried.

---

[51]Eusebius, V.21. According to tradition, https://www.catholic.org/saints/saint.php?saint_id=1499. The first judge was the praetorian prefect, a high-ranking aide to the emperor. The senate trial was conducted by a group of senators and judges.

When he would not deny his faith before the judge, his trial was moved to the Roman Senate.

At his senate trial, he presented an eloquent defense of the beauty and values of Christianity. However, he was condemned anyway. Apollonius was beheaded in about AD 185.

Copies of his defense document were widely shared among the early churches, but are now lost.

How would I defend my faith if I was grilled by senators? How would I explain the beauty and values of Christianity?

James (above) contrasted worldly wisdom and divine wisdom. Living with the righteous fruits of divine wisdom is certainly better than living with disorder and evil practices.

> PRAYER: Lord, thank you for heavenly wisdom. I will meditate on the beauty and good values of your kingdom. Then I will be ready to explain them to others. Amen.

37 Date of Easter

> And be kind and compassionate to one another, forgiving one another, just as God also forgave you in Christ.
> Ephesians 4:32 (CSB)

In the early centuries, Christians relied on the Jewish calendar to determine when to celebrate Easter. The churches in the West and in Egypt celebrated Easter on the Sunday following 14 Nissan of the

Defenders of the Faith, AD 100–200

Jewish calendar. The churches in the province of Asia, and others in the East, ended the Lenten fast on 14 Nissan irrespective of the day of the week. Alternative schemes were adopted in later centuries which did not rely on the Jewish calendar.

Those in the West felt it was important to always celebrate Easter on a Sunday. Those in the East felt synchronizing Easter and Jewish Passover was important. There were numerous letters and meetings to try to resolve this controversy.

In about AD 155, aged Polycarp, Bishop of Smyrna, visited Anicetus, Bishop of Rome.[52] They debated the issue of Easter's date and decided to disagree, but they shared communion together anyway.

Melito, Bishop of Sardis,[53] wrote about the date of Easter in the AD 160s. He strongly advocated the Eastern practice.

In about AD 193, Victor I, Bishop of Rome,[54] presided over a conference that validated the Western practice. A year later, Polycrates, Bishop of Ephesus, hosted a council in Ephesus that affirmed the Eastern practice. Victor was offended and excommunicated Polycrates and others. Victor was criticized for being so strict by other bishops in the West who did not break fellowship with the churches in

---

[52] Eusebius, V.23. According to tradition. Regarding Anicetus, Bishop of Rome, see https://www.catholic.org/saints/saint.php?saint_id=874.

[53] Regarding Melito, Bishop of Sardis, see https://www.catholic.org/saints/saint.php?saint_id=5068.

[54] Regarding Victor I, Bishop of Rome, see https://www.catholic.org/saints/saint.php?saint_id=843.

Date of Easter

the East.

Over the next hundred years or so, the controversy became less of an issue. Unity in the Spirit was more important.

Today, Christians are tolerant over the date of Easter. The Western denominations follow the Roman Catholic calendar which differs from the Eastern Orthodox calendar. These differences are due to events in later centuries.

The story of the Easter controversy helps me to react to controversies today with the same grace as Anicetus, Polycarp, and other early bishops. Sometimes fellow believers have differing ideas, so I must forgive them.

> PRAYER: Lord, let me react to controversies with humility, grace, and forgiveness. Amen.

Persecution and Toleration, AD 200-303

38 Heretics who Relied on Logic

> All Scripture is inspired by God and is profitable for teaching, for rebuking, for correcting, for training in righteousness, so that the man of God may be complete, equipped for every good work.
> 2 Timothy 3:16–17 (CSB)

In the early AD 200s, there were heretics among the Christians who did not respect the Old Testament Scriptures or the teachings received from the apostles.[55]

One group of heretics put logic and mathematics above the truth of the Scriptures. When confronted with a scriptural truth, they asked whether

---
[55]Eusebius, V.28. According to tradition.

Persecution and Toleration, AD 200–303

it can be put into a conjunctive or disjunctive syllogism of logic. They thought logic was the path to truth.

They studied the geometry of Euclid, the philosophy of Aristotle, and the science of Galen more than the Scriptures. Using the principles of unbelievers, they corrupted the simple faith of the gospel, and even claimed to have corrected it.

They eagerly copied the Scriptures, substituting their own ideas, thinking they were wiser than the Holy Spirit. The church fathers of that era, wrote many documents refuting such heresies.

Today, similar to those early heretics, there are some who claim to be Christians who think logic and science are the only reliable path to truth. They try to explain away miracles and the resurrection of Jesus. In effect, they elevate science into a religion.

Also like those early heretics, some today publish "translations" of the Bible and commentaries that substitute their ideas for what biblical manuscripts actually say. They twist the Bible to say whatever they want.

I have studied logic, mathematics, and science all my life. They all have limitations and cannot address the spiritual truths of the Bible. Logic cannot validate axioms and science cannot validate anything from insufficient data. But the Bible is a reliable foundation for a living faith and a relationship with God.

> PRAYER: Lord, thank you for the Bible, truth for following you. Amen.

39 Saint Narcissus, Bishop of Jerusalem

> "Fill the jars with water," Jesus told [the servants]. So they filled them to the brim. Then he said to them, "Now draw some out and take it to the headwaiter." And they did.
>
> When the headwaiter tasted the water (after it had become wine), he did not know where it came from—though the servants who had drawn the water knew. He called the groom and told him, "Everyone sets out the fine wine first, then, after people are drunk, the inferior. But you have kept the fine wine until now."
>
> John 2:7–10 (CSB)

Narcissus was the Bishop of Jerusalem for many years. He was famous for performing miracles.[56]

One year, the Christian community in Jerusalem celebrated an all-night vigil the night before Easter. During the night, the deacons ran out of oil for lamps. Everyone was deeply disturbed. Narcissus asked those tending the lamps to draw some water. He prayed over the water, and told them to pour it

---

[56] Eusebius, VI.9-10. According to tradition, https://www.catholic.org/saints/saint.php?saint_id=791. The date of this incident is uncertain. Narcissus became Bishop of Jerusalem in about AD 180. He died in about AD 216 at the age of about 117 years old.

into the lamps. The water became oil that burned through the night.

Jesus turned water into wine at a wedding banquet in Cana of Galilee to resolve an embarrassing situation. That first miracle was evidence he is the Messiah. In faith, Narcissus resolved a discouraging situation. It was evidence of the truth of the gospel believed by the Christians.

> PRAYER: Lord, when those around me are disturbed, I know you are the one to resolve the issue. Amen.

40 Saint Alexander, Bishop of Jerusalem

> During the night Paul had a vision in which a Macedonian man was standing and pleading with him, "Cross over to Macedonia and help us!" After he had seen the vision, we immediately made efforts to set out for Macedonia, concluding that God had called us to preach the gospel to them.
>
> Acts 16:9–10 (CSB)

Alexander was a bishop in the province of Cappadocia. In about AD 212, he made a pilgrimage to Jerusalem.[57]

---

[57]Eusebius, VI.11. According to tradition, https://www.catholic.org/saints/saint.php?saint_id=165. Narcissus died in about AD 216 at the age of 117. Alexander was martyred in about AD 251.

Saint Callistus I, Bishop of Rome

Due to his advanced age, Bishop Narcissus in Jerusalem was no longer able to fulfill the duties of bishop. The Christians in Jerusalem received a revelation to go out by a certain gate of the city to welcome the man who would be their bishop. Alexander arrived at that time.

Narcissus, the neighboring bishops, and the people confirmed Alexander's selection. So Alexander and Narcissus shared the office of bishop until Narcissus died a few years later.

Like the Christians in Jerusalem, Paul received a vision telling him and his companions where to go next (above). I too have had nudges from the Holy Spirit to go to certain places. In hindsight, I see that God had prepared appointments for me there.

> PRAYER: Lord, thank you for nudges from the Holy Spirit for the appointments you have prepared in advance for me. Amen.

41 Saint Callistus I, Bishop of Rome

> When the scribes who were Pharisees saw that [Jesus] was eating with sinners and tax collectors, they asked his disciples, "Why does he eat with tax collectors and sinners?"
>
> When Jesus heard this, he told them, "It is not those who are well who need a

> doctor, but those who are sick. I didn't come to call the righteous, but sinners."
>
> Mark 2:16–17 (CSB)

Callistus was a trusted slave of a Christian master in Rome.[58] However, Callistus made some unwise investments for his master and eventually was sentenced to forced labor in the mines of Sardinia with other banished Christians.

Some years after being released, he was ordained a deacon and became a close aide to Bishop Zephyrinus of Rome. When the bishop died in AD 217, Callistus became bishop.

As Bishop of Rome, Callistus showed mercy to repentant sinners, even those who had committed major sins. He allowed them into full communion with the Christian community. He even accepted those who crossed class boundaries, such as marriages between free masters and slaves. Similarly, he accepted those who repented of heresy and schism.

Callistus understood that the mission of Jesus was calling sinners to repent and that Christians must do the same. He also knew Christians must forgive others, because in Christ, God has forgiven each of us.

> PRAYER: Lord, increase my compassion for those caught in sin so that I can welcome repentant believers from sinful backgrounds. Amen.

---

[58] According to tradition, https://www.catholic.org/saints/saint.php?saint_id=31. Callistus was martyred in about AD 222.

42 Saints Theodore and Athenodore

> Study to shew thyself approved unto God, a workman that needeth not to be ashamed, rightly dividing the word of truth.
>
> 2 Timothy 2:15 (KJV)

In about AD 233, as young men, Theodore and his brother Athenodore studied with Origen in Caesarea, Palestine.[59] Origen was the most famous theologian of his time.

In the beginning, they were fascinated by Greek and Roman philosophy. Origen instilled in them passion for divine truth instead of pagan things.

When I was in high school and college, I studied the famous philosophers and classic literature of Western Civilization. I found out the Scriptures made much more sense, explaining human nature. Now I have a passion for divine truth, like Theodore and Athenodore.

Today we have more resources than Theodore and Athenodore had for studying the Scriptures. The search feature of an on-line translation is like a concordance. An academic commentary explains differences among ancient manuscripts, the nuances of the original languages, and the customs of ancient cultures. We now have a wealth of theology commentaries by believers.

---

[59] Eusebius, VI.30. Theodore and Athenodore later became bishops in the region of Pontus. Theodore was later known as "Gregory, the Wonderworker."

When I study the Scriptures, I may read more than one translation. I may consult academic commentaries. I don't want a simple mistake to lead me into a heresy. But most of all, I want to apply the Bible to my life.

> PRAYER: Lord, point out the Scriptures that are important for me to apply today. Amen.

43 Persecution by Maximinus, the Thracian

> Preach the word; be ready in season and out of season; correct, rebuke, and encourage with great patience and teaching.
>
> 2 Timothy 4:2 (CSB)

When Maximinus, the Thracian, became emperor in AD 235, he ordered that Christian leaders be executed, because they were the ones who taught the gospel.[60] Maximinus was hostile to the household of his predecessor, the Emperor Alexander Severus, which included Christians, so he attacked all Christians. Maximinus's reign lasted about three years.

A pastor or a ministry leader has a public platform. Everyone knows who the preacher is. When the gospel is offensive to the world, a teacher is an easy target. A pastor may be slandered, arrested,

---
[60]Eusebius, VI.28.

and jailed for standing up for righteousness. The mission is clear, but teaching the Word of God without compromise can be dangerous.

When I teach the Bible in public, post on social media, or publish this book, I'm risking backlash from the world.

> PRAYER: Lord, give me boldness to speak and write in season and out of season. Amen.

44 Saint Pontian, Bishop of Rome

> There is one body and one Spirit—just as you were called to one hope at your calling—one Lord, one faith, one baptism, one God and Father of all, who is above all and through all and in all.
> Ephesians 4:4–6 (CSB)

Pontian became bishop of Rome in about AD 230.[61] He was opposed during his reign by Hippolytus and his faction. When Emperor Maximinus, the Thracian, ordered a persecution in AD 235, both Pontian and Hippolytus were arrested and sentenced to hard labor in the mines of Sardinia.

After he was sentenced, Pontian resigned as bishop, so a new bishop could be promptly named. His resignation meant a new bishop would care for

---

[61] According to tradition, https://www.catholic.org/saints/saint.php?saint_id=882.

his flock while he was in exile. Selecting a new bishop also ended a schism in the church at Rome. While working in Sardinia, Pontian and Hippolytus were reconciled. They both died within a year due to the conditions there.

Pontian was mindful of the need for unity among Christians. Believers are unified into one body by many aspects of our faith: one Spirit, one hope, one faith, one baptism, one Lord, and one God the Father. When I meditate on each of these, it is clear that factions are not God's way.

> PRAYER: Lord, I will cultivate unity among believers and love for one another. Amen.

45 Saint Gregory, the Wonderworker

> Be strengthened by the Lord and by his vast strength. Put on the full armor of God so that you can stand against the schemes of the devil.
> Ephesians 6:10–11 (CSB)

Gregory was from the city of Neocaesarea in the region of Pontus.[62] After becoming a Christian in

---

[62] *The Life of Gregory the Wonderworker*, by Gregory of Nyssa, written about AD 380. https://www.lectio-divina.org/images/nyssa/Gregory%20the%20Wonderworker.pdf. See https://www.catholic.org/saints/saint.php?saint_id=656. Gregory, the Wonderworker, is also known as "Gregory Thaumaturgus," "Gregory of Neocaesarea," and "Theodore."

Saint Gregory, the Wonderworker

Palestine, he wanted to evangelize his native region.

In about AD 238, he and a few companions set out to return to Neocaesarea. When an evening thunderstorm arose near a certain city in Pontus, they took shelter in a pagan temple. As usual, they spent the night praying and singing hymns, and then they left at dawn.

The temple-warden was accustomed to receiving oracles from a demon in this temple. However, that morning the demon let him know that he could not enter due to Gregory's prayers. The temple-warden tried various pagan rites to invite the demon without success.

The temple-warden found Gregory and demanded that he let the demon back into the temple. So Gregory wrote a note: "Gregory to Satan: Enter." The temple-warden put the paper on the pagan altar and the demon returned.

After learning more about God's power, the temple-warden became a Christian and many in that city believed. Gregory served as bishop of Neocaesarea and became famous for working miracles.

Praying through the night was Gregory's customary practice. Nothing unusual happened that night, it seemed, but the demon could not withstand God's presence. Like Gregory, I have spiritual armor and God's power which defeats demons.

> PRAYER: Lord, I will rely on your spiritual power and armor. Demons are not intimidating. Amen.

46 Saint Fabian, Bishop of Rome

> As soon as [Jesus] came up out of the water, he saw the heavens being torn open and the Spirit descending on him like a dove. And a voice came from heaven: "You are my beloved Son; with you I am well-pleased."
>
> Mark 1:10–11 (CSB)

In about AD 238, Anteros, Bishop of Rome, died after serving only a month. Fabian, an ordinary layman, came with others from the countryside to Rome to see the selection of the next bishop.[63]

All the Christians in Rome gathered together to make the selection. There were many well known leaders there that people were considering. Suddenly, a dove descended from above and landed on Fabian's head. Mindful of the dove that descended on Jesus, the whole assembly shouted, "He is worthy!" and immediately, they made Fabian bishop.

The Christians in Rome considered the dove on Fabian to be a divine sign of God's choice. Whenever a new leader must be chosen for any group of believers, obeying the direction of the Holy Spirit is the most important criterion. Denominations and local churches may have established procedures, but sensitive attention to the leading of the Holy Spirit is always the goal.

---

[63] Eusebius, VI.29. According to tradition, https://www.catholic.org/saints/saint.php?saint_id=47. Fabian was martyred in about AD 250.

PRAYER: Lord, guide me whenever I am involved in choosing leaders. Amen.

47 Saint Alexander, Bishop of Comana

> All of you clothe yourselves with humility toward one another, because
> > God resists the proud
> > but gives grace to the humble.
> >
> > 1 Peter 5:5 (CSB)

Alexander was an ordinary Christian layman in the city of Comana in the region of Pontus. He wanted a humble lifestyle, so he made charcoal, a very low-class dirty occupation.[64]

When Comana needed a bishop, Gregory, the Wonderworker, came to town to select the bishop.[65] Gregory was the bishop of Neocaesarea at that time, and oversaw the region of Pontus. Gregory interviewed many candidates without success.

Someone jokingly suggested Alexander, the charcoal-burner. Gregory called Alexander and interviewed him. He found that Alexander was a wise virtuous man, so Gregory selected him to be bishop of the city.

---

[64] Wood is burned to create charcoal.

[65] According to tradition, https://www.catholic.org/saints/saint.php?saint_id=1247. Alexander, Bishop of Comana, was martyred in about AD 251. See also *The Life of Gregory the Wonderworker*, by Gregory of Nyssa, which mentions this incident. https://www.lectio-divina.org/images/nyssa/Gregory%20the%20Wonderworker.pdf.

I admire Alexander's humility. He did not seek elevation to bishop. He was just living a humble life. Pride is a natural human attitude, but humility is important in the kingdom of God. I certainly need the grace God gives the humble.

> PRAYER: Lord, search my heart for pride. My desire is to become more humble. Amen.

48 Persecution by Decius

> [Jesus said,] "You will even be brought before governors and kings because of me, to bear witness to them and to the Gentiles. But when they hand you over, don't worry about how or what you are to speak. For you will be given what to say at that hour, because it isn't you speaking, but the Spirit of your Father is speaking through you."
> Matthew 10:18–20 (CSB)

Emperor Philip, the Arab, married a Christian and was sympathetic toward the believers. When Decius became the next emperor in AD 249. He persecuted the Christians because of hatred for his predecessor.[66] He also blamed the problems of the empire on the lack of worship for the pagan gods.

The persecution was systematic and empire-wide. Decius required everyone to perform an act

---

[66]Eusebius, VI.39. Maier, pp. 225–226.

of pagan worship to receive a certificate, but many Christians refused to worship idols and had to explain why they refused. Decius died in battle after reigning for about two years.

Jesus promised that the Holy Spirit would give believers words to say when on trial for the gospel. Whenever worldly people want me to explain why I don't participate in their activities, the Holy Spirit will give me the right response.

> PRAYER: Lord, thank you for your promise to speak through me in difficult situations. Amen.

49 Saint Dionysius, Bishop of Alexandria

> We know that all things work together for the good of those who love God, who are called according to his purpose.
> Romans 8:28 (CSB)

In about AD 249, the Emperor Decius ordered persecution of the Christians. When his edict was proclaimed in Alexandria, Egypt, the governor sent soldiers to arrest Dionysius, the bishop.[67] The soldiers searched everywhere he might be hiding without success, while Dionysius waited at home.

---

[67]Eusebius, VI.40. Eusebius quoted a letter by Dionysius himself. See also https://www.catholic.org/saints/saint.php?saint_id=2905. Dionysius died in about AD 265.

Persecution and Toleration, AD 200–303

After four days, some Christian brothers took Dionysius to a house in the countryside, but around sunset, soldiers found them and arrested the group. Because it was late, they rested for the night in a nearby village.

One of the brothers named Timothy was absent. Arriving at the empty house, he learned from servants where they had gone. As Timothy fled, a villager asked him why he was in such a hurry. Timothy told him. The villager was on his way to an all-night wedding feast, and so he told all the wedding guests what had happened to the bishop.

Everyone at the feast arose and went to the house where the soldiers were keeping Dionysius. Faced with a hostile crowd, all the soldiers fled. Dionysius was rescued.

Dionysius and a group of Christians then spent the persecution at a remote village in the Libyan desert, and when it was safe, they returned to the city.

Dionysius experienced one divine coincidence after another. He was ready to be arrested in Alexandria, but the soldiers couldn't find him. The brothers insisted that he leave the city, so he went with them. His arrest was too late in the day to return to the city. Timothy happened to be absent. The villager was curious when he saw Timothy. There happened to be a wedding feast that night, and the wedding guests intimidated the soldiers, so they fled. All these divine coincidences resulted in his rescue.

God arranges coincidences for me, like he did for Dionysius.

PRAYER: Lord, thank you for working out all things for my good. Amen.

50 Saint Felix of Nola

> How great is your goodness,
> which you have stored up
> for those who fear you.
> In the presence of everyone
> you have acted
> for those who take refuge in you.
> You hide them in the protection
> of your presence;
> you conceal them in a shelter
> from human schemes,
> from quarrelsome tongues.
>   Psalm 31:19–20 (CSB)

Felix was a Christian from near Nola, Italy.[68] When his father died, he sold most of his inherited land and gave to the poor. He became an assistant to Maximus, Bishop of Nola.

When persecution arose in about AD 250, Maximus fled to the countryside. Felix was arrested in his place, but escaped from prison. He was then directed by the Holy Spirit where to find Maximus who was alone, sick, and helpless. Felix brought him back to town, and together they hid from the authorities.

---

[68] According to tradition, https://www.catholic.org/saints/saint.php?saint_id=639.

Persecution and Toleration, AD 200–303

At one point, they hid in a vacant building. A spider quickly spun a web over the door, which fooled the soldiers into thinking the building was long abandoned, so they didn't go inside.

A few years later, after the bishop's death, Felix refused to become the bishop, recommending a senior priest. Felix then farmed what remained of his land, sharing with the poor. He died of old age in about AD 260.

Felix and Maximus experienced the protection of the Lord that the psalmist David wrote about. I haven't needed to hide from soldiers, like they did, but the Lord is there to help in every difficult situation.

> PRAYER: Lord, thank you for your presence which protects me from schemes and quarrels. Amen.

51 Saints Abdon and Sennen

> Daniel spoke with the king [Darius]: "May the king live forever. My God sent his angel and shut the lions' mouths; and they haven't harmed me, for I was found innocent before him. And also before you, Your Majesty, I have not done harm."
>
> Daniel 6:21–22 (CSB)

Abdon was a Persian Christian. Sennen was his companion. In about AD 250, during the persecution by the Emperor Decius, they were arrested and taken as prisoners to Rome.[69]

Receiving death sentences, they were put in an arena, and then hungry wild animals were let loose. The animals refused to hurt them. In frustration, the authorities sent in gladiators, who killed them with the sword.

Abdon and Sennen experienced a miracle like the prophet Daniel. Their plight was similar to other martyrs. Execution by ferocious animals in an arena was used throughout the empire as entertainment for the pagan populace. Some Christians were killed by wild beasts, but others were left unharmed.

If I have to face a hostile crowd or an unjust government for the faith, I'll remember Abdon and Sennen. Modern persecution may not use wild beasts or gladiators, but the faith of the martyrs is still needed today.

> PRAYER: Lord, I trust you when I face opposition. Amen.

52 Saint Agatha of Sicily

> Timothy, my son, I am giving you this instruction in keeping with the prophecies previously made about you, so that

---

[69] According to tradition, https://www.catholic.org/saints/saint.php?saint_id=1071. Information about Abdon's and Sennen's lives is very limited.

Persecution and Toleration, AD 200–303

by recalling them you may fight the good fight, having faith and a good conscience.

1 Timothy 1:18–19 (CSB)

During the early centuries, there were many women throughout the empire who took courageous stands for the faith. Many were young virgins who refused to marry a pagan suitor. As a result, they were tortured and martyred. The details of their stories varied, but they all demonstrated faith and endurance.

Agatha of Sicily was one such virgin.[70] She became a Christian at a young age. By age fifteen, she had vowed to remain a virgin and to dedicate her life to serving Christ. Thus, she refused the marriage proposals of a high-ranking suitor.

During the persecution by the Emperor Decius, she was arrested and the judge turned out to be her spurned suitor. Failing to convince her to marry him, he sent her to confinement at a brothel. When that didn't persuade her to marry him, he sent her to prison where she was tortured. She died in prison from her wounds in about AD 251.

Agatha had wholehearted devotion to Jesus, even when facing severe persecution. She refused to marry a pagan and live a comfortable life because of her loyalty to Christ. She fought the good fight of faith.

PRAYER: Lord, I want to be fully devoted to following you. Amen.

---

[70] According to tradition, https://www.catholic.org/saints/saint.php?saint_id=14.

53 Saint Christopher

> Just as each one has received a gift, use it to serve others, as good stewards of the varied grace of God.
>
> 1 Peter 4:10 (CSB)

Christopher became a Christian when he found out that Jesus, the King of Kings, is the most powerful king in the world. Because he was a large man, Christopher volunteered to help travelers ford a dangerous river as his service to Christ.[71]

One day, a child, asked for his help to cross the river. Christopher carried the child on his shoulders. As they crossed, the child became very heavy. With great effort, Christopher and the child reached the shore. Christopher asked the child why he became so heavy. The child answered that he was Christ and he had the whole world on his shoulders. Then the child vanished.

Christopher chose a humble way to serve Jesus. He found something he could do to help others. God has given every believer abilities that can serve others.

While serving by carrying the child, Christopher experienced an encounter that illustrates the weighty love Jesus has for all mankind. Because of his love, he bore the sins of everyone on the cross.

PRAYER: Lord, thank you for your

---

[71] According to tradition, https://www.catholic.org/saints/saint.php?saint_id=36. Christopher was martyred in about AD 251.

54 Serapion, the Repentant

> This punishment by the majority is sufficient for that person [who publicly sinned]. As a result, you should instead forgive and comfort him. Otherwise, he may be overwhelmed by excessive grief. Therefore I urge you to reaffirm your love to him.
> 2 Corinthians 2:6–8 (CSB)

Serapion was an elderly Christian in Alexandria, Egypt, who had lived blamelessly most of his life. However, he lapsed during the persecution by the Emperor Decius, publicly sacrificing to an idol.[72]

He pleaded for forgiveness to church leaders, but no one paid him attention. He became sick and was unconscious for three days. On the fourth night, when he revived briefly, he knew he was about to die. So, he called his grandson, and said, "Go and get one of the presbyters" (elders).

The grandson ran to a presbyter, but the presbyter was ill and could not go. The bishop had given instructions for such cases. So the presbyter

---

[72]Eusebius, VI.44. Eusebius quoted a letter by Dionysius, Bishop of Alexandria. This incident occurred sometime after AD 251. Serapion was a believer, but is not honored as a "Saint" today.

gave the boy a piece of Eucharist bread and told him to soak it and let it fall drop by drop into his grandfather's mouth.

The boy returned and did as the presbyter had instructed. When his grandfather had swallowed a little, he died at peace.

Serapion's public sin of sacrificing to an idol was wiped away, and he was reconciled to the local Christian community. After his death, he was recognized by the local Christians for all his good deeds.

Paul wrote to the believers in Corinth to discipline a member who had sinned publicly (incest). The member repented, so in his second letter to Corinth, Paul told them to forgive and comfort him (above). Similarly, Serapion was forgiven and comforted by the presbyter's action.

> PRAYER: Lord, give me your compassion to forgive and comfort those who have repented of public sin. Amen.

55 Persecution by Valerian

> First of all, then, I urge that petitions, prayers, intercessions, and thanksgivings be made for everyone, for kings and all those who are in authority, so that we may lead a tranquil and quiet life in all godliness and dignity.
> 1 Timothy 2:1–2 (CSB)

Persecution and Toleration, AD 200–303

In AD 251, Gallus succeeded Decius as emperor and continued persecuting Christians. He banished Christian leaders who were praying for the welfare of his reign.[73]

In AD 253, Valerian and his son became co-emperors. Early in his reign, Valerian was friendly toward the Christians. Even many of his household were believers. However, an adviser persuaded him to persecute and kill Christians throughout the empire and to participate in occult practices.

After Valerian was captured in battle by the Persians in AD 260, his son Gallienus became sole emperor and ended the persecution.

The early Christians followed the guidance in Paul's letter to Timothy (above) to pray for the welfare of all in authority, including the emperor. However, the emperors and governors despised the blessings that came from the believers' prayers and exiled the ones who were praying for their benefit.

Like those Christian leaders, I will pray for the government officials over me, federal, state, and local.

> PRAYER: Lord, I pray for truth, righteousness, and justice in our land, so that believers can lead peaceful godly lives. I pray that government officials will make righteous decisions. Amen.

---

[73]Eusebius, VII.1,10–13.

56 Saint Saturninus, Bishop of Toulouse

> Submit to God. Resist the devil, and he will flee from you. Draw near to God, and he will draw near to you.
>
> James 4:7–8 (CSB)

Saturninus was an effective evangelist in the province of Gaul. He became bishop in the city of Toulouse where his flock met in a small church building.[74]

The most important pagan temple in the city was a place where demons gave oracles to the priests. Whenever Saturninus walked from his home to the church building, this temple was along his path. As he passed by, the demons could not speak. This angered the pagan priests.

One day in about AD 257, the priests saw him going by, grabbed him, and demanded that he sacrifice to the pagan gods. He boldly refused. Burning with anger they tied his feet to a raging bull which dragged him through the streets of the city, killing him.

Saturninus was just minding his own business as he walked by the temple day after day. Nothing unusual seemed to happen. But the demons could tell he was walking by, and they were silenced. The God of the universe was with Saturninus.

Like Saturninus, if I submit to God and draw near to him, demons can't influence me or those

---

[74] According to tradition, https://www.catholic.org/saints/saint.php?saint_id=802.

around me. If I notice the devil at work and resist him, he will flee, because the one true God is present.

> PRAYER: Lord, I submit to you in all that I do. Your presence is where I want to be. Amen.

57 Exile of Saint Dionysius, Bishop of Alexandria

> As soon as it was night, the brothers and sisters [in Thessalonica] sent Paul and Silas away to Berea. Upon arrival, they went into the synagogue of the Jews. The people here were of more noble character than those in Thessalonica, since they received the word with eagerness and examined the Scriptures daily to see if these things were so. Consequently, many of them believed, including a number of the prominent Greek women as well as men.
> Acts 17:10–12 (CSB)

During the persecution by Emperor Valerian, in about AD 258, Dionysius, Bishop of Alexandria, Egypt, a presbyter (elder), and three deacons were arrested and tried.[75] The deputy governor tried to

---

[75] Eusebius, VII.11. Eusebius quoted a letter by Dionysius himself. https://www.catholic.org/saints/saint.php?saint_id=2905. Dionysius died in AD 265.

Exile of Saint Dionysius, Bishop of Alexandria

persuade them to worship the pagan gods in addition to the Christian God. They told him they worshiped the one true God, so the deputy governor banished them to a village in Libya and forbade the Christians from holding assemblies.

At the village in Libya, a large church formed, drawing from a wide area. Some came from the city and some from elsewhere in Egypt. Even some local pagans were converted. It seemed like a mission from God.

Later the deputy governor exiled groups of Christians to various villages in Libya. He moved Dionysius to another rougher village, but this village was close to a highway and closer to Alexandria. Christians from Alexandria came to spend the night and enjoy local assemblies there. This allowed Dionysius to give some pastoral oversight to those he loved in the city. The persecution ended a few years later.

Even though Dionysius was being punished, the first village turned out to be a successful evangelistic mission, and the second village was a base for pastoring.

What looked like punishments, were actually spiritual opportunities for Dionysius. Even though Paul and Silas were forced out of Thessalonica, Berea was receptive. Sometimes what looks like persecution moves one to a fruitful place for evangelism and service.

God knows where I need to be. Sometimes he uses adverse circumstances to get me there.

PRAYER: Lord, Thank you for using circumstances to move me where I need to be. Amen.

58 Saint Lawrence of Rome

> Instruct [those who are rich] to do what is good, to be rich in good works, to be generous and willing to share, storing up treasure for themselves as a good foundation for the coming age, so that they may take hold of what is truly life.
> 1 Timothy 6:18–19 (CSB)

During the persecution by the Emperor Valerian, when someone was condemned, their wealth was confiscated by the emperor.

In about AD 258, Sixtus II, Bishop of Rome, was martyred. Lawrence was the deacon in charge of the money and valuable items of the church.[76] So the emperor's official demanded that Lawrence surrender the treasures of the church. Lawrence asked for three days to gather the wealth, which was granted.

During the three days, Lawrence gave away church money and valuables to the poor, crippled, and blind throughout the city as fast as he could. He asked them to gather at a certain place.

---

[76] According to tradition, https://www.catholic.org/saints/saint.php?saint_id=366. It is uncertain whether Lawrence appeared before the city prefect or the emperor himself.

After three days, Lawrence appeared before the official. When ordered to deliver the treasures of the church, Lawrence brought in the crowd of poor people and said, "Behold the treasures of the church which I promised to show you. You see, the church is truly rich, far richer than your emperor."

This enraged the official. Lawrence was promptly martyred.

Jesus honored the poor everywhere he went. Lawrence understood that the poor are a valuable part of Christ's body. They are "treasures of the church." Paul told Timothy to teach rich believers to be generous to the poor (above). So Lawrence was generous.

> PRAYER: Lord, teach me how to be more generous. How can I show respect to the poor I encounter? Amen.

59 Repentant from Heresy

> [Walk] with all humility and gentleness, with patience, bearing with one another in love, making every effort to keep the unity of the Spirit through the bond of peace.
> Ephesians 4:2–3 (CSB)

Due to the many heresies that had arisen, there was controversy among the bishops over what to do when someone repents of a heresy. Some refused reconciliation; some required rebaptism; some required a public act of penance of some kind; some

Persecution and Toleration, AD 200–303

required laying-on-of-hands; and some just welcomed the repentant.[77]

Cyprian, Bishop of Carthage,[78] insisted on rebaptism of the repentant. Churches in the eastern provinces also rebaptized the repentant.

Dionysius, Bishop of Alexandria,[79] said their established custom was public renunciation of the heretical teaching by the repentant, followed by prayer and laying-on-of-hands. Stephen, Bishop of Rome,[80] strongly agreed.

Dionysius had a faithful member who realized his baptism years earlier was based on heresy, so he wanted to be rebaptized the correct way. Dionysius ruled the fact he had affirmed his faith many times over the years sufficed, so the community continued to embrace him without rebaptism.

Sixtus II, Bishop of Rome,[81] believed baptism was a once-in-a-lifetime event, but advocated toleration of those bishops who rebaptized. He restored relations with the bishops in the African and eastern provinces which had been broken off by his predecessor bishop, Stephen.

Controversies among believers arise from time

---

[77]Eusebius, VII.2–9. Eusebius quoted several letters by Dionysius, Bishop of Alexandria, regarding repentants from heresy and rebaptism.

[78]Cyprian became bishop of Carthage in about AD 248 and was martyred in about AD 258.

[79]Dionysius became bishop of Alexandria in about AD 247 and died in about AD 265.

[80]Stephen became bishop of Rome in about AD 254 and was martyred in about AD 257.

[81]Sixtus II became bishop of Rome in about AD 257 and was martyred in in about AD 258.

to time. Sometime there are strong opinions, like Stephen's. Tolerance for the other side is often necessary, like Sixtus showed. Grace should be extended to those caught in the middle, like Dionysius gave his faithful member.

I must love my Christian brother, even when he has mistaken ideas, and even if he is stubborn and won't listen to my "persuasive arguments." To maintain unity, my "persuasive arguments" must be delivered with humility, gentleness, patience, and love. After all, I might be wrong myself.

> PRAYER: Lord, show me how to keep unity of the faith with my difficult brothers. Amen.

60 Saint Fructuosus, Bishop of Tarragona

> Pray at all times in the Spirit with every prayer and request, and stay alert with all perseverance and intercession for all the saints.
>
> Ephesians 6:18 (CSB)

Fructuosus was bishop of the city of Tarragona in the province of Hispania.[82] During the persecution by the Emperor Valerian, in about AD 259, Fructuosus and two of his deacons were arrested and condemned by the governor.

---

[82] According to tradition, https://www.catholic.org/saints/saint.php?saint_id=3478.

Persecution and Toleration, AD 200–303

On the way to his death in the arena, some Christians gathered at its gate and asked for his prayers. He replied loudly, "I am bound to bear in mind the whole universal church from east to west." He also comforted those gathered nearby. Fructuosus felt compelled to pray for all Christians.

Fructuosus and the other martyrs prayed with outstretched arms as the flames rose around them.

Today, we hear news from around the world. There is plenty to pray about. I have friends who live in other countries; I especially pray for them. I pray for believers in difficult situations, even if I don't know them personally.

> PRAYER: Lord, I intercede for believers everywhere, especially those facing persecution. Amen.

61 During the Plague

> [Jesus said:] This is my command: Love one another as I have loved you. No one has greater love than this: to lay down his life for his friends.
> John 15:12–13 (CSB)

In about AD 250, a plague broke out and spread across the Roman empire for the next fifteen years.[83] Perhaps in about AD 260, Bishop Dionysius

---
[83]Maier, p. 239. Eusebius VII.22. Eusebius quoted a letter by Dionysius, Bishop of Alexandria.

During the Plague

wrote a letter describing how the plague affected Alexandria, Egypt.

The plague was extremely contagious. People were dying everywhere. The pagans were so afraid of the plague they fled from the sick, even abandoning family members. The unburied were treated without respect, like garbage on the roadside.

The Christians suffered from the plague like everyone else, but showed love and loyalty to the sick. They tended the sick, even though they knew they might become infected. Church leaders lost their lives this way. Some would prepare corpses for a Christian burial only to be buried themselves soon after. These Christians were like martyrs.

In 2020, the world was hit by the COVID-19 pandemic. Many were afraid for themselves and their loved ones. Guidance from health officials was confusing. It was a difficult time.

Believers were affected like everyone else. They found ways to care for the sick, to connect with those who were isolated, and to fellowship anyway.

> PRAYER: Lord, fill me with your love and compassion for the sick and hurting. I will give practical help, even in the middle of a pandemic. Amen.

62 Saint Dionysius, Bishop of Rome

> Now about the collection for the saints: Do the same as I instructed the Galatian churches... When I arrive, I will send with letters those you recommend to carry your gift to Jerusalem.
> 1 Corinthians 16:1–3 (CSB)

The church in Rome became disorganized by the persecution of Emperor Valerian. Bishop Sixtus was martyred in about AD 258. When the persecution subsided somewhat, Dionysius was elected bishop of Rome the next year.[84] (This Dionysius is different from Dionysius, Bishop of Alexandria.) After the persecution ended in about AD 260, Dionysius worked to bring order to the church in Rome, establishing leaders, places of worship, cemeteries, and other properties.

During this time, he heard about devastation of churches in the province of Cappadocia by marauding bands of Goths. So he sent large sums of money to Cappadocia to ransom church members and rebuild churches.

Dionysius followed the example of Paul by providing relief for Christians in another province. In Paul's time, there was a famine in Palestine, so Paul organized a collection of money for the believers in Jerusalem. In his letter (above), he told the

---

[84] According to tradition, https://www.catholic.org/saints/saint.php?saint_id=2909. Dionysius, Bishop of Rome, died in about AD 268.

church in Corinth, Greece, to prepare gifts weekly, so the money would be ready when he arrived. The church in Corinth then appointed couriers who took the the gift to Jerusalem.

From time to time today, special needs arise among Christians whom I can help. In 2005, Hurricane Katrina devastated the Gulf coast of the United States. I saw the churches in northern Mississippi immediately send money, supplies, and workers to help. The roads south were spontaneously full of pickup trucks loaded with supplies, grills, generators, chainsaws, and other equipment. They went wherever they could find someone in need, without being told what to do.

> PRAYER: Lord, guide me to when and where I should contribute to relief efforts. Amen.

63 Saint Astyrius

> So the great dragon was thrown out [of heaven]—the ancient serpent, who is called the devil and Satan, the one who deceives the whole world. He was thrown to earth, and his angels with him.
> Revelation 12:9 (CSB)

There were springs in Caesarea Philippi which were headwaters of the Jordan River. During a certain festival, the pagans would throw a human sacrifice into the gushing spring. Due to a demon's power, the body would disappear into the spring. The pagans considered this a miracle.

Astyrius was a Roman senator who was a devout Christian[85] and lived in nearby Caesarea, Palestine. He happened to be in Caesarea Philippi during this festival and observed how the people were deceived by the demon. So he prayed to God through Christ to defeat the demon. Suddenly, the sacrifice's body floated to the surface. The marvel never happened again.

Astyrius recognized that the people were not worshiping the true God, the creator of the universe. They had been deceived by the marvel of the demon. So Astyrius prayed.

Satan and his demons are deceivers. God's power reveals the truth and defeats their deception.

> PRAYER: Lord, show me when people around me are deceived by Satan's forces. Like Astyrius, I will pray for Satan's defeat. Amen.

64 Saint Marinus

> [Jesus said,] "If anyone wants to follow after me, let him deny himself, take up his cross, and follow me. For whoever wants to save his life will lose it, but whoever loses his life because of me and

---

[85]Eusebius, VII.16–17. According to tradition, https://www.catholic.org/saints/saint.php?saint_id=6020. Astyrius was martyred in Caesarea, Palestine, in about AD 262.

Saint Marinus

> the gospel will save it. For what does it benefit someone to gain the whole world and yet lose his life?"
>
> Mark 8:34–36 (CSB)

Marinus was a Roman army officer who was a Christian.[86] He was stationed in Caesarea, Palestine. In about AD 262, he was honored to be next in line for promotion to centurion, but another soldier complained that Marinus was disqualified, because he would not offer sacrifices to the emperor.

The governor examined Marinus who declared his faith in Christ. The governor then gave Marinus three hours to reconsider.

During this time, Bishop Theotecnus took Marinus to a nearby church and asked him to choose between his sword and a book of the Gospels. Marinus reached for the book. So, the bishop encouraged him and said, "Go in peace."

When Marinus returned to the governor, he had even greater zeal for the gospel. So he was promptly beheaded.

Today, like Marinus, a believer must sometimes choose between promotion by the world and the gospel. Following Jesus may mean foregoing a lucrative career path. It always means denying my selfish interests. Eternal life is more valuable than all the rewards of a worldly lifestyle.

> PRAYER: Lord, I choose to follow you. Amen.

---

[86]Eusebius, VII.15. According to tradition, https://www.catholic.org/saints/saint.php?saint_id=6020.

65 Saint Anatolius of Laodicea, Syria

> Who can separate us from the love of Christ? Can affliction or distress or persecution or famine or nakedness or danger or sword? … No, in all these things we are more than conquerors through him who loved us.
>
> Romans 8:35,37 (CSB)

Anatolius, a Christian, was a famous scholar of mathematics and science in Alexandria, Egypt.[87]

A rebellion against the Romans arose in the Greek part of Alexandria where Anatolius lived. The Roman army besieged the rebels, and as a result, the residents were starving.

Eusebius, a deacon in Alexandria, (not the author of the *Church History*) had favor with the Roman general. So Anatolius proposed through Eusebius that deserters from the rebel side be welcomed by the Romans, and the commander agreed.

On the rebel side, Anatolius proposed to let anyone useless for fighting leave, and the rebels agreed. However, Anatolius then arranged for all the Christians to leave first, followed by anyone else who wanted to leave. They were all welcomed by Deacon Eusebius on the Roman side who cared for

---

[87]Eusebius, VII.32. According to tradition, https://www.catholic.org/saints/saint.php?saint_id=1381. In about AD 268, while passing through the city of Laodicea in the province of Syria, the Christians there made Anatolius bishop. Anatolius died in about AD 283.

them like a father. The rebellion collapsed soon after.

God used Anatolius and Deacon Eusebius to break the famine for whoever wanted to leave the rebelling district. God's love often overcomes affliction through the actions of believers.

> PRAYER: Lord, make me an instrument of your love to those who are hurting. Amen.

66 Saint Valentine of Rome

> [Jesus read from Isaiah:] The Spirit of the Lord is on me, because he has anointed me to preach good news to the poor. He has sent me to proclaim release to the captives and recovery of sight to the blind, to set free the oppressed, to proclaim the year of the Lord's favor.
> Luke 4:18–19 (CSB)

Valentine was a priest in Italy.[88] Today he is widely celebrated on February 14, Valentine's Day.

Valentine was arrested for his faith. During his trial, Valentine and the judge discussed religion and faith. When Valentine presented the gospel about Jesus, the judge immediately put him to a test.

---

[88] According to tradition, https://www.catholic.org/saints/saint.php?saint_id=159. Valentine was martyred in about AD 269 in Rome.

Persecution and Toleration, AD 200–303

The judge presented Valentine with his blind daughter and told him to restore her sight. If he succeeded, the judge promised to do anything Valentine requested. So Valentine put his hands on her eyes, and she was healed.

Fulfilling his promise, the judge broke all the idols in his home, fasted three days, was baptized, and released all the Christian prisoners under his authority. All forty-four members of his household were baptized.

The passage Jesus read from Isaiah (above) was his mission as the Messiah. It included healing the blind, which he did many times. Valentine did the same thing Jesus had done.

> PRAYER: O Lord, I must rely on you for answers to life's challenges. You are faithful. Amen.

67 Saint Castulus

> Don't neglect to show hospitality, for by doing this some have welcomed angels as guests without knowing it.
> Hebrews 13:2 (CSB)

Castulus was a chamberlain of the Emperor Diocletian in Rome.[89] Being a Christian, he sheltered fellow Christians in his home and hosted religious

---
[89] According to tradition, https://www.catholic.org/saints/saint.php?saint_id=583.

services in the palace. That was the last place the authorities would look for Christians.

In about AD 286, he was betrayed by a disgruntled Christian, tried, tortured, and executed. His wife Irene buried him and was later martyred also.

Castulus was a generous host. His home was a safe house for Christian fugitives due to his position. His workplace had plenty of room for meetings. He did not neglect hospitality. Perhaps some of his guests were angels.

My wife and I may not work for an emperor, but generous hospitality is an attitude we can express anywhere. Like the home of Castulus, our home is a place for helping others.

> PRAYER: Lord, show me creative ways to extend hospitality to believers. Amen.

68   Saints Comas and Damian

> If anyone serves, let it be from the strength God provides, so that God may be glorified through Jesus Christ in everything.
>
> 1 Peter 4:11 (CSB)

Cosmas and Damian were Christian twin brothers, born in Arabia, who became accomplished medical physicians in the port city of Aegeae in the province of Cilicia.[90]

They practiced medicine and surgery without charging a fee. This attracted many to the faith. They were credited with curing many kinds of ailments, and were highly esteemed by the populace of the city.

In about AD 287, the governor arrested them, because of their fame as Christian healers. The governor ordered them to renounce their faith, but they remained true. After enduring tortures, they were beheaded.

Comas and Damian served their community using their medical knowledge, wisdom, and skill. They demonstrated their love for their patients by serving for free. The cures may have seemed natural, but they probably prayed over all their patients, too.

The practice of medicine is uncertain. A treatment or medicine often only helps some people and not others. Which one should a doctor prescribe? I have known Christian doctors who decided what medicine to prescribe with help from the Holy Spirit. What they prescribed worked for me.

> PRAYER: Lord, thank you for Christian medical professionals who apply your principles with their medical training and pray for their patients. Amen.

---

[90] According to tradition, https://www.catholic.org/saints/saint.php?saint_id=471.

69 Saint Sebastian

> [Jesus said,] "Don't be afraid of them, since there is nothing covered that won't be uncovered and nothing hidden that won't be made known... Don't fear those who kill the body but are not able to kill the soul."
>
> Matthew 10:26–28 (CSB)

Sebastian was a young Christian from the province of Gaul, who joined the Roman army, hoping to help fellow Christians.[91] Due to his courage and excellent service, he was promoted to the Praetorian Guard, who were bodyguards for the emperor.

While serving in the Praetorian Guard, he converted several prominent people to the faith. As a result, the authorities found out he was a Christian. The Emperor Diocletian reprimanded him and condemned him to death. They tied him to a stake and archers used him for target practice.

The archers filled his body with arrows and left him for dead. Irene of Rome recovered his body for burial, but discovered he was still alive. She nursed him back to health at her home.

After his recovery, in about AD 288, Sebastian searched for a way to confront the emperor about his unjust persecution of Christians. He surprised the emperor in a stairwell. After the shock of seeing someone he thought was dead, the emperor ordered that Sebastian be beaten to death with clubs.

---

[91] According to tradition, https://www.catholic.org/saints/saint.php?saint_id=103.

Persecution and Toleration, AD 200–303

Sebastian had risked being discovered when he had presented the gospel to prominent people, because his job was close to the pagan emperor. After surviving archery target practice, he was not afraid of what the emperor could do to him, so he pursued justice for fellow Christians. Risking death, he knew his soul was secure.

Because I'm a believer, I can confidently go into risky situations where God leads me, knowing hidden things will be revealed and my soul is secure.

> PRAYER: Lord, give me ideas for pursing justice and give me your protection in dangerous situations. Amen.

70 Saints Primus and Felician

> In fact, all who want to live a godly life in Christ Jesus will be persecuted. Evil people and impostors will become worse, deceiving and being deceived. But as for you, continue in what you have learned and firmly believed.
> 2 Timothy 3:12–14 (CSB)

Primus and his younger brother Felician were Christians living in a suburb of Rome.[92] They devoted their lives to helping the poor and visiting Christian prisoners.

---

[92] According to tradition, https://www.catholic.org/saints/saint.php?saint_id=5802. Primus was eighty years old when he was martyred.

Saints Primus and Felician

In their old age, about AD 297, they were arrested for refusing to participate in the usual sacrifices to the pagan gods. Several times, they were tortured separately and then asked again to sacrifice which each of them refused.

Eventually, Primus was beheaded. Then the judge tried to deceive Felician, telling him that his elder brother Primus had offered the sacrifice. Felician recognized that this was a lie, and remained steadfast in his faith. So he was beheaded the same day as his brother.

Even though many Christians had renounced their faith when tortured, Felician knew the faith of his brother. They had a lifetime of doing good works together. They had risked their lives together. They had refused to participate in civic festivals together. The judge was obviously an evil man. Paul told Timothy (above) to expect deception from such men. The judge's tale was clearly a lie. Felician knew the truth.

The world is a confusing place when I try to live a godly life. Worldly people try to get their way through deception, but like Felician, I can continue in the way of truth, following Jesus.

> PRAYER: Lord, help me to recognize the lies of the world. I will remain faithful in spite of opposition. Amen.

71 Saints Cassian of Tangier and Genesius of Arles

[Isaiah prophesied,] "Here is my servant whom I have chosen, my beloved in whom I delight; I will put my Spirit on him, and he will proclaim justice to the nations."

Matthew 12:18 (CSB)

Marcellus, the Centurion,[93] was a soldier stationed in the city of Tangier in the province of Hispania. He was a Christian, and in about AD 298, he dramatically refused to celebrate the birthday of Augustus Maximian, who ruled under the Emperor Diocletian. The celebration included sacrifices to pagan gods. Marcellus was immediately arrested.

Cassian was a pagan court recorder in Tangier.[94] His job was to transcribe the testimony and verdicts at trials. While recording the trial of Marcellus, Cassian grew angry at the injustice of the charge. When the death sentence was declared, he threw down his pen and declared that the sentence was unjust. He was immediately arrested and promptly martyred.

Similarly, Genesius was a court recorder in the

---

[93] According to the tradition of Saint Marcellus, the Centurion, https://en.wikipedia.org/wiki/Marcellus_of_Tangier. Tangier is located in modern Morocco. The province of Hispania consisted of modern Spain, Portugal, and Morocco at this time.

[94] According to the tradition of Saint Cassian of Tangier, https://www.catholic.org/saints/saint.php?saint_id=2620.

city of Arles in the province of Gaul.[95] He was a new Christian convert preparing for baptism. In about AD 303, he was required to transcribe the edict ordering persecution of Christians. He could not write the words, so he threw down his implements and immediately resigned. He fled, but was caught and martyred.

Apparently, the testimony of Marcellus convinced Cassian to become a Christian. Cassian and Genesius took a stand for justice. Matthew quoted Isaiah 42:1 about Jesus, the Messiah (above). When Jesus returns, he will rule the nations with justice.

Living in the kingdom of God today means I know what is just and unjust. In America, we have many ways to press for justice without getting martyred. Sometimes a private word is all that is needed. Sometimes a public protest is necessary.

> PRAYER: Lord, I will stand for justice whenever the occasion arises. Amen.

72 Saint Andrew, the Tribune

> And what more can I say? Time is too short for me to tell about Gideon, Barak, Samson, Jephthah, David, Samuel, and the prophets, who by faith conquered kingdoms, … escaped the edge of the

---

[95] According to the tradition of Saint Genesius of Arles, https://www.catholic.org/saints/saint.php?saint_id=5868.

> sword, gained strength in weakness, became mighty in battle, and put foreign armies to flight... Others experienced mockings and scourgings, as well as bonds and imprisonment.
>
> Hebrews 11:32–36 (CSB)

Andrew was a high-ranking officer in the Roman army, a tribune, stationed in the province of Syria.[96]

In about AD 300, his small detachment of pagan soldiers was confronted by a large Persian force. He prayed to Christ for aid. Then they went into battle and routed the enemy. As a result, Andrew and some of his soldiers became Christians.

When they victoriously returned to Antioch, Andrew was denounced for being a Christian and for converting soldiers under his command. The governor discharged Andrew and his group of Christians from the army, and then tried them, imprisoned them, and executed some.

The governor wrote to the emperor asking whether to impose the death sentence. The emperor knew the army loved Andrew, so he decided to free them, but secretly ordered their execution on a different pretext. Andrew and his group fled to the city of Tarsus in the province of Cilicia to be baptized. They then fled into the Taurus Mountains. The Roman army ambushed them, killing Andrew and all of the former soldiers who were with him, about 2,600.

---

[96] According to tradition, https://www.catholic.org/saints/saint.php?saint_id=1400.

Saint Fabius

I don't know when Andrew heard about the God of the Christians, but going into battle, he reached out to Christ. The results convinced him and many of his soldiers to convert. Upon returning to Antioch, their faith was tested.

Hebrews chapter eleven summarizes the faith of various heroes in the Old Testament (above). Andrew and his soldiers were similar to some who had gone before, winning battles, enduring scourgings, imprisonment, and escaping the sword for a time. Finally, they were martyred for their faith.

> PRAYER: Lord, thank you for men of faith who endured testing. I want to be faithful like they were when I am tested. Amen.

73 Saint Fabius

> Little children, guard yourselves from idols.
> 1 John 5:21 (CSB)

Fabius was a Roman soldier in the province of Mauretania (modern Algeria) who was a Christian.[97]

In about AD 300, the governor planned a meeting which included a pagan ceremony. Fabius was given the honor of carrying the governor's banner which depicted pagan images and was involved in the pagan worship. Even though other soldiers

---

[97] According to tradition, https://www.catholic.org/saints/saint.php?saint_id=3640.

Persecution and Toleration, AD 200–303

were participating, Fabius knew he should avoid idol worship, so he refused to carry the banner.

After torture in prison, the authorities tried to convince him to change his mind, but he remained steadfast, so he was beheaded.

Today, an idol is anything that I might give my complete loyalty. My peers might pressure me to participate in their schemes, but I must remain completely loyal to the Lord.

> PRAYER: Lord, help me recognize the idols of our culture and to resist peer pressure to join in. Amen.

74 Before the Great Persecution

> The Lord disciplines the one he loves
> and punishes every son he receives.
> Hebrews 12:6 (CSB)

From AD 260 to 303, the Christians were somewhat tolerated by the Roman government.[98] The Christian community grew and prospered throughout society. However, within the churches, pride, envy, and factions sprang up, and corrupt leaders fought for power with each other. Discipline by the Lord was inevitable and the pagan Emperor Diocletian was to be the instrument.

Christians are subject to discipline by the Lord, individually and corporately. The Lord disciplined Israel in the Old Testament. Similarly, the Lord has

---
[98] Eusebius, VIII.1.

Before the Great Persecution

disciplined his people and their leaders when there were patterns of sin and corruption. Church history is a warning to leaders of churches and ministries today.

PRAYER: Lord, even though your discipline through circumstances today is sometimes necessary, thank you for your loving care for believers. Amen.

The Great Persecution, AD 303-313

75 The Great Persecution by Diocletian

> Dear friends, don't be surprised when the fiery ordeal comes among you to test you, as if something unusual were happening to you. Instead, rejoice as you share in the sufferings of Christ, so that you may also rejoice with great joy when his glory is revealed.
> 1 Peter 4:12–13 (CSB)

Diocletian became emperor in AD 285. He divided administration of the empire into four parts. By AD 303, he and Maximian ruled the East and West respectively, each with the title "Augustus." Under them, Galerius and Constantius Chlorus ruled parts of the East and West, each with the title "Caesar."

Diocletian tolerated the Christians early in his reign, but in AD 303, he began the Great Persecution

The Great Persecution, AD 303–313

empire-wide.[99] He ordered destruction of church buildings, burning of Bibles, and torture and execution of whoever would not worship the pagan gods.

Caesar Constantius Chlorus minimized the effect of the persecution edicts in his domain, but Caesar Galerius pursued a raging campaign of death and destruction in the East, searching for Christians city-to-city and house-to-house.

Diocletian abdicated as Augustus in AD 305, but the persecution continued in the East under his successor, Galerius.

The Great Persecution was certainly a fiery ordeal. The many martyrs will rejoice when Jesus returns. Like the early Christians, believers are attacked in various places around the world today.

> PRAYER: Lord, I pray for your mercy and strength for believers who are being persecuted today by mobs and governments around the world. Amen.

76 Soldiers

> [Jesus said,] "Peace I leave with you. My peace I give to you. I do not give to you as the world gives. Don't let your heart be troubled or fearful.
> John 14:27 (CSB)

Shortly after the edict was published in AD 303, Caesar Galerius began the Great Persecution by

---
[99]Eusebius, VIII.2. Maier, pp. 283–285.

Saint George

sorting soldiers in the army. Commanders let soldiers choose either to conform to the edict or to disobey. If they made pagan sacrifices, they kept all the privileges of their rank. If they refused, they were stripped of rank and discharged, becoming poor civilians.[100]

Many soldiers gladly chose to become civilians instead of renouncing their faith in Christ. The glory and prosperity of military life did not compare to belonging to Christ's kingdom. A few soldiers were also martyred for their faith.

Today, a Christian may be faced with the same choice as these soldiers. One may be offered a promotion with a big salary which requires long hours, working on Sundays, and perhaps unethical business practices. All these pressures amount to worshiping the company. Refusal might mean being black-listed and difficulty finding the next job.

Following Jesus and living in the kingdom of God was more valuable than the privileges of a Roman soldier. The peace Jesus gives is better than the benefits of worshiping the company.

> PRAYER: Lord, thank you for guiding my career and for all the benefits of living in your kingdom. Amen.

77 Saint George

Then war broke out in heaven: Michael and his angels fought against the

---
[100]Eusebius, VIII.4

dragon. The dragon and his angels also fought, but he could not prevail, and there was no place for them in heaven any longer.

Revelation 12:7–8 (CSB)

George was raised by Christian parents who were Greeks from Lydda, Palestine. He followed them in the faith. When he was old enough, he joined the Roman army.[101]

A dragon (or crocodile) took up residence in a spring that served the pagan city of Silene, Libya. It prevented the people of the city from getting water. So, they offered a sheep each day to get the dragon temporarily away from the spring. When they ran out of sheep, they decided to offer a maiden each day. One day, George arrived at the city. He killed the dragon before the ruler's daughter could be eaten. As a result, the people converted to Christ.

Later, George was promoted in the army to serve as a bodyguard for the emperor. In AD 303, the Emperor Diocletian required everyone in the army to sacrifice to the pagan gods. George refused and was martyred.

The story of George defeating a dragon reminds me of the ultimate battle with a dragon. In Revelation chapter 12 (above), Satan is represented by a dragon. In his vision, John saw war in heaven between God's angels and the dragon's forces. The

---

[101] According to tradition, https://www.catholic.org/saints/saint.php?saint_id=280. There are several versions of the story of George killing a dragon. This one became very popular in Europe in medieval times.

dragon and his demons were defeated and cast out of heaven. He can no longer accuse God's people. Today, he is busy deceiving people, trying to make them reject the gospel.

> PRAYER: Lord, help me recognize the deceptions of Satan and to present your truth to others. Amen.

78 Saint Genesius of Rome

> For the word of the cross is foolishness to those who are perishing, but it is the power of God to us who are being saved.
> 1 Corinthians 1:18 (CSB)

Genesius was leader of a theatrical troupe in Rome.[102] He pretended to be a new convert to learn about Christian beliefs and practices. He then wrote a play that mocked Christianity and baptism, in particular.

In about AD 303, the Emperor Diocletian visited Rome and Genesius performed his play, knowing that the emperor hated Christians. During the performance, Genesius played a believer being baptized and another actor played the priest. As the "priest" poured water over him, Genesius encountered Christ and became convinced of the truth of

---
[102] According to tradition, https://www.catholic.org/saints/saint.php?saint_id=185.

The Great Persecution, AD 303–313

the gospel. In front of everyone, he preached the Christian faith and confronted the emperor. The emperor was enraged and demanded Genesius renounce his newfound faith. When he refused, he was promptly tortured and beheaded.

Genesius originally thought the Christians were fools, easy targets for a comedy. He thought his play would gain the emperor's favor. But the king of the universe intervened. Genesius experienced God's power for salvation.

Today, an atheist may mock Christians like Genesius did, but the gospel is true. Faith in Christ opens the door to life now and for eternity.

> PRAYER: Lord, thank you for true wisdom, power for living, and a relationship with you for eternity. Amen.

79 Saint Felix, Bishop of Thibiuca

> I have treasured your word in my heart
> so that I may not sin against you
> Lord, may you be blessed;
> teach me your statutes.
> With my lips I proclaim
> all the judgments from your mouth
> I rejoice in the way revealed by your decrees
> as much as in all riches.
> I will meditate on your precepts
> and think about your ways.

Saint Felix, Bishop of Thibiuca

> I will delight in your statutes;
> I will not forget your word.
> Psalm 119:11–16 (CSB)

Felix was bishop of the city of Thibiuca in the province of Africa.[103]

In AD 303, the Emperor Diocletian's edict to persecute the Christians included the command to burn the Scriptures. So the city's magistrate demanded that Felix surrender the church's copies of the Scriptures and other sacred books. Felix refused. He was arrested and sent to Carthage with others where they were all beheaded.

Before the invention of the printing press, books were copied by hand. A Christian congregation had to share a precious copy of the Scriptures. Felix knew the importance of their copy of the Scriptures for the spiritual life of his people. He gave his life for them. Even today, Bibles are contraband in some parts of the world.

In most countries today, Bibles are plentiful in printed and electronic forms. Translations are available in many languages. Anyone can read it every day. Memorizing Bible verses implants their message in my soul. Then I'm ready to explain the gospel whenever needed, even if a Bible is not handy.

> PRAYER: Lord, thinking about your Word is my delight. I will be diligent to remember your teaching. Amen.

---

[103] According to tradition, https://www.catholic.org/saints/saint.php?saint_id=3676.

80 Saint Erasmus, Bishop of Formia

> [Elihu spoke:] Listen to this, Job. Stop and consider God's wonders. Do you know how God directs his clouds or makes their lightning flash?
> Job 37:14–15 (CSB)

Erasmus, also known as Elmo, was bishop of Formia, Italy.[104]

While Erasmus was preaching outdoors, a lightning bolt hit the ground near him. He kept preaching in spite of the storm, trusting God for his safety.

This incident resulted in his name being associated with Saint Elmo's Fire, a natural weather phenomenon. During thunderstorms at night, sailors sometimes saw a glow at the tip of the ship's mast and called it Saint Elmo's Fire. They considered it a sign of protection by God.

Erasmus was unshakable in his faith during persecution. After being imprisoned, tortured, and escaping several times, he was martyred in about AD 303.

Erasmus stood in faith in spite of dangerous circumstances. I'll imitate his faith, but I'll take shelter in thunderstorms.

> PRAYER: Lord, whenever I see lightning, I will remember the faith of Erasmus. Amen.

---

[104] According to tradition, https://www.catholic.org/saints/saint.php?saint_id=182.

81 Saint Luxorius

> How happy is the one who does not
> walk in the advice of the wicked
> or stand in the pathway with sinners
> or sit in the company of mockers!
> Instead, his delight is in the Lord's instruction,
> and he meditates on it day and night.
>
> Psalm 1:1–2 (CSB)

Luxorius was a pagan assistant to the provincial governor of the island of Sardinia.[105] As part of his official duties, he acquired a copy of the Old Testament Scriptures. He became interested in the Psalms. Reading them convinced him to become a Christian. So he began to pray, to deny idols, and to study the Scriptures.

In about AD 303, due to a complaint, he was arrested and appeared before the governor. The governor accused him of betraying his trust in him as his assistant, because he would not obey the emperor's orders. He steadfastly refused to sacrifice to the pagan gods, and so he was beheaded.

Perhaps the first verses of the Psalms (above) caught the attention of Luxorius. Nobody wants to associate with the wicked, sinners, or mockers. Everyone wants to experience happiness and delight. What is the path to that delight? Meditating on the Word of God, the Christian Scriptures, is the way.

---

[105] According to tradition, https://www.catholic.org/saints/saint.php?saint_id=4371.

As a young believer, I started to read through the Bible. Studying the Bible has been the foundation for my gradual spiritual growth.

> PRAYER: Lord, thank you for your Word, and especially for the Psalms. Amen.

82 Saint Pantaleon

> The [prodigal] son said to him, 'Father, I have sinned against heaven and in your sight. I'm no longer worthy to be called your son.' But the father told his servants, 'Quick! Bring out the best robe and put it on him; put a ring on his finger and sandals on his feet.'
> Luke 15:21–22 (CSB)

Pantaleon was the son of a pagan father and a Christian mother in the imperial city of Nicomedia in the region of Bythinia.[106] He followed the faith of his mother, but after her death, he fell away. While studying medicine under a famous physician and then while serving in the court of Augustus Maximian, he gave up his Christian faith completely.

He was won back to Christ by a priest who convinced him that Jesus was a better physician and was the way of salvation. After he repented, he distributed his wealth to the poor and cared for the

---

[106] According to tradition, https://www.catholic.org/saints/saint.php?saint_id=373.

sick without charge. Several miraculous healings are attributed to him.

In about AD 303, Pantaleon was denounced for his faith by envious colleagues in the imperial court, and after a trial, was martyred.

Many young people today follow the faith of their parents in their teen years, but fall away in college or when starting their careers. The parable of the Prodigal Son (above) teaches us that God welcomes those who repent, like Pantaleon did. Salvation then motivates one to be kind and to do good works.

> PRAYER: Lord, thank you for welcoming me when I repented of my sins. Amen.

83 Saint Phocas, the Gardener

> For I [Paul] am already being poured out as a drink offering, and the time for my departure is close. I have fought the good fight, I have finished the race, I have kept the faith. There is reserved for me the crown of righteousness, which the Lord, the righteous Judge, will give me on that day, and not only to me, but to all those who have loved his appearing.
>
> 2 Timothy 4:6–8 (CSB)

Phocas was a Christian who lived just outside the

The Great Persecution, AD 303–313

city of Sinope in the region of Pontus.[107] He earned his living by cultivating a garden. He was well-known for helping the poor and opening his home to travelers.

In about AD 303, because he was a well-known Christian, soldiers were sent to execute him. They arrived near Sinope and needed a place to spend the night. Phocas welcomed them into his home and fed them. When he found out their mission, he promised to lead them to Phocas in the morning. While the soldiers slept, he dug a grave for himself.

In the morning, he told the soldiers, "Phocas is found."

The soldiers asked, "Where is he?"

He led them to the grave and answered, "I am the man."

The soldiers were shocked. Phocas explained his hope for eternal life. When the soldiers saw that he was willing, they beheaded him. He was buried in the grave he had prepared.

Paul told Timothy he was ready for execution (above). He had a reward waiting for him. A believer's hope for eternal life means death is not intimidating.

> PRAYER: Lord, thank you for assurance of eternal life. Amen.

---

[107] According to tradition, https://www.catholic.org/saints/saint.php?saint_id=5449.

84 Saints Felix and Adauctus

> We know that "an idol is nothing in the world," and that "there is no God but one."
>
> 1 Corinthians 8:4 (CSB)

> So then, my dear friends, flee from idolatry.
>
> 1 Corinthians 10:14 (CSB)

Felix was a priest in Rome.[108] In about AD 304, he was arrested and tried by a city official.

Felix was taken to the temple of Serapis and was ordered to sacrifice to the god. At his prayer, the idol fell and shattered. Then they took him to the temple of Mercury and again ordered him to sacrifice to the god. At his prayer, the idol fell and shattered. Then they took him to the temple of Diana. Again, at his prayer, the idol fell and shattered. Frustrated, they led him away to be executed.

On the way, an unknown person joined him, and declared he was a Christian. They were both beheaded. The local Christians named him Adauctus, the Latin word for "added."

Today, most people don't worship statues. However, there are many idols in modern society. Anything that captivates a person's attention, loyalty, and devotion is an idol, such as money, ca-

---

[108] According to tradition, https://www.catholic.org/saints/saint.php?saint_id=3684.

reer, music, sports, politics, sex, personal appearance, recreation, or hobbies.

A Christian's sincere gentle testimony can shatter someone's idol, demonstrating that it is not very significant. Such superficial things in life do not deserve my rapt attention, loyalty, and devotion. Only God deserves my worship.

> PRAYER: Lord, you are the focus of my worship. Modern idols are nothing compared to you. Amen.

85 Saints Marcellinus and Peter

> But as for you, exercise self-control in everything, endure hardship, do the work of an evangelist, fulfill your ministry.
> 2 Timothy 4:5 (CSB)

Marcellinus was a priest in Rome and Peter was an exorcist.[109] In about AD 304, they were arrested and imprisoned. These two saw going to jail as another opportunity for evangelism. They converted their jailer and his family.

At their trial, the magistrate condemned them to death. He wanted to deny them a proper burial, so he ordered that they be secretly executed in a forest

---

[109] According to tradition, https://www.catholic.org/saints/saint.php?saint_id=77.

several miles from Rome. In the forest, they happily cleared briers, thorns, and thickets. They were beheaded and buried there. Two Christian women, guided by the Holy Spirit, found their graves and had them properly buried. An executioner became a Christian later.

Marcellinus and Peter did the work of evangelists, even when facing hardship. They fulfilled their ministry. I will apply Paul's advice to Timothy (above) to my life like they did. I will develop self-control, endure difficult times, and win others to Jesus. Obeying the Holy Spirit will result in completing God's plan for me.

> PRAYER: Lord, I am committed to following your path for me. I want to lead others to you, like Marcellinus and Peter did. Amen.

86 Beasts in the Arena

> We are afflicted in every way but not crushed; we are perplexed but not in despair; we are persecuted but not abandoned; we are struck down but not destroyed.
> 2 Corinthians 4:8–9 (CSB)

For hundreds of years, the Romans released wild beasts in arenas to kill people as a spectacle for the populace. Gladiators, criminals, and Christians faced leopards, panthers, bears, wild boars, and

The Great Persecution, AD 303–313

bulls goaded by hot irons. This was done throughout the empire.

In AD 303, the Christians were attacked in the city of Tyre in the province of Phoenicia. Eusebius personally saw the courage of the Christians and the power of God at work in the arena at Tyre.[110]

When a beast rushed toward a certain Christian, it suddenly stopped and retreated, astonishing the crowd. When the first beast did nothing, they released a second and a third against the same martyr.

A teenager stood unbound alone in the arena praying with his arms stretched wide. Bears and panthers came up to his face, snarling death, but they didn't hurt him.

A group of five Christians were supposed to be attacked by a raging bull, but the bull attacked those trying to goad it. The bull pawed his hooves and thrust his horns at the Christians, but he was harmless.

When execution by beasts did not work, the frustrated authorities killed the martyrs with the sword.

Many others across the empire were martyred in arenas. Today, we may not have all their stories, but we admire their faith.

Even though I may not face wild beasts in an arena, I may need courage to stand for my Lord, like the martyrs did. The grace of God is there for me whenever afflicted, perplexed, persecuted, or struck down.

---

[110]Eusebius, VIII.7.

PRAYER: Lord, you are my source of strength for every challenge. Amen.

87 Saint Adrian of Nicomedia

What no eye has seen, no ear has heard, and no human heart has conceived— God has prepared these things for those who love him.

1 Corinthians 2:9 (CSB)

Adrian of Nicomedia was a soldier in the imperial court of Augustus Galerius in the city of Nicomedia, in the region of Bythinia.[111]

In about AD 306, while supervising the torture of some Christians, he asked what reward they expected to receive. They replied, quoting 1 Corinthians 2:9 (above). Amazed at their hope and courage, he and his wife Natalia became Christians.

When he publicly confessed his faith, he was immediately imprisoned, tortured, and then executed.

Believers have hope for eternal life and amazing benefits from God. No jail, torture, or even execution can take that away. Adrian and Natalia experienced this hope themselves when by faith they became Christians.

PRAYER: Lord, thank you for all the things you have prepared for me and those who love you. Amen.

---

[111] According to tradition, https://www.catholic.org/saints/saint.php?saint_id=253.

The Great Persecution, AD 303–313

88 Saint Peter, Bishop of Alexandria

> Above all, put on love, which is the perfect bond of unity.
>
> Colossians 3:14 (CSB)

Peter became Bishop of Alexandria, Egypt, in about AD 300 and survived the persecution by the Emperor Diocletian.[112] He ruled that anyone who repented of sacrificing to idols could be accepted back into the Christian community after proper penance.

Melitius and his faction vehemently opposed Peter. They thought he was too lenient. Melitius insisted on rebaptism of those who lapsed. This controversy disrupted the church in Alexandria for many years.

When persecution resumed in AD 306, after Diocletian had abdicated, Peter was forced into exile, but he encouraged his flock with his letters. Peter returned to the city in about AD 311 and was soon martyred by the Roman authorities.

Peter was dedicated to the spiritual welfare of his flock. He embraced those who repented after the time of persecution. However, factions among the local Christians made the bond of unity difficult.

Today, factions often hinder love and unity among believers. Disagreements over theology, leadership, and tradition have resulted in the many denominations we have today.

---

[112] According to tradition, https://www.catholic.org/saints/saint.php?saint_id=5376.

The End of Persecution

> PRAYER: Lord, give me your love for those with mistaken ideas, those who follow flawed leaders, and those who value traditions I disagree with. Amen.

89 The End of Persecution

The eyes of the Lord are on the righteous and his ears are open to their prayer. But the face of the Lord is against those who do what is evil.

1 Peter 3:12 (CSB)

After about ten years of severe persecution, in AD 312, Constantine, the son of Constantius Chlorus, became Augustus in the West when he defeated his rival, Maxentius, son of Maximian, in the famous Battle of Milvian Bridge.[113]

In AD 313, Constantine and Licinius, the Augustus in the East, jointly issued the Edict of Milan, which granted toleration to all religions empire-wide, ending all the persecution. In AD 324, Constantine became the sole emperor.

During the Great Persecution, the Christians prayed for deliverance. The Lord heard their prayer and answered by giving success to the Emperor Constantine.

The Lord is attentive to the prayers of believers around the world today, some of whom face persecution like the early Christians.

---

[113] Eusebius, IX.9–11. Maier, pp. 304–306.

PRAYER: Lord, I ask for deliverance from persecution for those suffering today. Amen.

90 Martyrs

> When [the Lamb] opened the fifth seal, I saw under the altar the souls of those who had been slaughtered because of the word of God and the testimony they had given. They cried out with a loud voice, "Lord, the one who is holy and true, how long until you judge those who live on the earth and avenge our blood?" So they were each given a white robe, and they were told to rest a little while longer until the number would be completed of their fellow servants and their brothers and sisters, who were going to be killed just as they had been.
> Revelation 6:9–11 (CSB)

In his vision, John saw the Lamb take a seven-sealed scroll, break the seals one by one, and open the scroll bit by bit. When the fifth seal was broken, John saw the souls of those who had been martyred under the heavenly altar. They cried out to the Lord for justice. They were told to be patient, because there were going to be more martyrs. Their company was not yet complete.

The end of persecution in the Roman empire in AD 313 did not end the killing of believers. Over

Martyrs

the centuries, there have been many more martyrs. Today, there are many places where Christians are routinely murdered for the faith. They are martyrs. Persecution of Christians today may also take the form of personal violence, arrests, imprisonment, arson of churches, and shootings in schools or during worship services.

When I hear news of persecution, I pray for God's grace for those suffering. When Jesus returns, he will be the righteous judge of the perpetrators.

> PRAYER: Lord, comfort those who are facing severe persecution today. Like the martyrs under the altar, I pray for your justice. Amen.

Index

A Lame Man, 1
Augustus Licinius, 123
Augustus Maximian, 105

Beasts in the Arena, 119
Before the Great Persecution, 102
Bible reference
  Job
    37:14–15, 112
  Psalm
    1:1–2, 113
    31:19–20, 69
    119:11–16, 110
  Daniel
    6:21–22, 70
  Matthew
    5:10, 22
    5:11–12, 15
    5:44, 9
    10:1,7, 4
    10:18–20, 66
    10:26–28, 95
    10:32–33, 17
    12:18, 98
    24:15–16, 20
    28:19–20, 11
  Mark
    1:10–11, 64
    2:16–17, 57
    8:34–36, 88
    13:11, 24
    16:15–17, 42
    16:15–18, 39
  Luke
    4:18–19, 91
    10:9, 10
    15:21–22, 114
  John
    2:7–10, 55
    7:37–39, 16
    14:27, 106
    15:12–13, 84
    16:1–2, 43
  Acts
    3:1–4:22, 1
    3:8, 1

Index

6:8–8:1, 3
7:58; 8:1, 2
8:26–39, 6
8:27–28, 6
10:1–2, 7
10:1–48, 7
12:1–2, 9
14:3, 40
15:6–21, 13
15:6–29, 34
15:28–29, 33
16:9–10, 56
17:10–12, 78
23:12–27:1, 13
28:16,30–31, 18

Romans
 8:28, 67
 8:35,37, 90

1 Corinthians
 1:18, 109
 2:9, 121
 8:4, 117
 10:14, 117
 16:1–3, 86

2 Corinthians
 2:6–8, 74
 4:8–9, 119

Ephesians
 4:2–3, 81
 4:4–6, 61
 4:11–12, 21
 4:29, 27
 4:32, 49

6:10–11, 62
6:18, 83

Colossians
 2:8, 36
 3:14, 122

1 Timothy
 1:18–19, 71
 2:1–2, 75
 6:11–12, 37
 6:18–19, 80

2 Timothy
 2:15, 47, 59
 3:12–14, 96
 3:16–17, 53
 4:2, 60
 4:5, 32, 118
 4:6–8, 18, 115

Hebrews
 1:8, 31
 10:23, 19
 11:32–36, 99
 12:6, 102
 13:2, 92
 13:15–16, 28

James
 1:1, 13
 3:16–18, 48
 4:7–8, 77
 5:16–18, 45
 5:19–20, 25

1 Peter
 2:12, 29
 3:12, 123

Index

    3:15, 34
    4:10, 73
    4:11, 93
    4:12–13, 105
    5:5, 65
1 John
    4:1, 44
    5:21, 101
Revelation
    1:9, 23
    6:9–11, 124
    12:7–8, 107
    12:9, 87

Caesar Constantius Chlorus, 105
Caesar Galerius, 105

Date of Easter, 49
During the Plague, 84

Emperor Constantine, 123
Emperor Decius, 66
Emperor Diocletian, 105
Emperor Domitian, 23
Emperor Maximinus, the Thracian, 60
Emperor Nero, 15
Emperor Trajan, 30
Emperor Valerian, 76
Ethiopian Eunuch, 6

Exile of Saint Dionysius, Bishop of Alexandria, 78

Flee from Jerusalem, 20

Grandsons of Jude, 24

Heretics who Relied on Logic, 53

Martyrs, 124
Melitene Soldiers, 45

Persecution by Decius, 66
Persecution by Domitian, 22
Persecution by Maximinus, the Thracian, 60
Persecution by Nero, 15
Persecution by Valerian, 75
Persecution in Gaul, 43
Persecution Reduced by Trajan, 29
Pliny, the Younger, 30

Index

Repentant from
    Heresy, 81

Saint Abercius,
Bishop of Hieropolis,
42
Saint Acestes, 18
Saint Adrian
of Nicomedia, 121
Saint Agatha
of Sicily, 71
Saint Alexander,
Bishop of Comana, 65
Saint Alexander,
Bishop of Jerusalem,
56
Saint Anacletus,
Bishop of Rome, 21
Saint Anatolius
of Laodicea, Syria, 90
Saint Andrew,
the Tribune, 99
Saint Anianus,
Bishop of Alexandria,
10
Saint Anicetus,
Bishop of Rome, 50
Saint Apollonius,
the Apologist, 48
Saint Astyrius, 87
Saint Athenodore, 59
Saint Callistus I,
Bishop of Rome, 57

Saint Castulus, 92
Saint Christopher, 73
Saint Cornelius,
the Centurion, 7
Saint Cyprian,
Bishop of Carthage,
82
Saint Dionysius,
Bishop of Alexandria,
67, 74, 78, 82, 84
Saint Dionysius,
Bishop of Rome, 86
Saint Erasmus,
Bishop of Formia, 112
Saint Eudokia
of Heliopolis, 28
Saint Fabian,
Bishop of Rome, 64
Saint Fabius, 101
Saint Felix,
Bishop of Thibiuca,
110
Saint Felix
of Nola, 69
Saint Fructuosus,
Bishop of Tarragona,
83
Saint Genesius
of Arles, 98
Saint Genesius
of Rome, 109
Saint George, 107
Saint Getulius, 32

Index

Saint Gregory,
the Wonderworker,
62, 65
Saint Hermias
of Comana, 39
Saint Hyacinth
of Caesarea, 33
Saint Ignatius,
Bishop of Antioch, 27
Saint Irenaeus,
Bishop of Lyon, 44
Saint James,
the Apostle, 9
Saint James,
the Just, 13
Saint John,
the Apostle, 1, 23, 25
Saint Justin Martyr, 36
Saint Lawrence
of Rome, 80
Saint Leucius,
Bishop of Brindisi, 40
Saint Luxorius, 113
Saint Marinus, 88
Saint Mark,
the Evangelist, 10
Saint Martinian, 16
Saint Melito,
Bishop of Sardis, 50
Saint Narcissus,
Bishop of Jerusalem,
55
Saint Pantaenus,
the Philosopher, 47
Saint Pantaleon, 114
Saint Peter,
Bishop of Alexandria,
122
Saint Peter,
the Apostle, 1, 8
Saint Philip,
the Deacon, 6
Saint Phocas,
the Gardener, 115
Saint Polycarp,
Bishop of Smyrna, 37,
50
Saint Pontian,
Bishop of Rome, 61
Saint Pothinus,
Bishop of Lyon, 45
Saint Quadratus
of Athens, 34
Saint Romulus, 31
Saints Abdon
and Sennen, 70
Saint Saturninus,
Bishop of Toulouse,
77
Saints Cassian of
Tangier
and Genesius of
Arles, 98
Saints Comas
and Damian, 93
Saint Sebastian, 95

Index

Saints Felix
and Adauctus, 117
Saint Sixtus II,
Bishop of Rome, 80, 82
Saints Marcellinus
and Peter, 118
Saints Primus
and Felician, 96
Saints Processus
and Martinian, 16
Saint Stephen,
Bishop of Rome, 82
Saints Theodore
and Athenodore, 59
Saint Thaddeus, 4
Saint Thomas,
the Apostle, 5, 11
Saint Torpes
of Pisa, 17
Saint Ursicinus
of Ravenna, 19
Saint Valentine
of Rome, 91
Saint Victor I,
Bishop of Rome, 50
Saul of Tarsus, 2
Serapion,
the Repentant, 74
Soldiers, 106

The End of Persecution, 123
The Great Persecution
by Diocletian, 105

About the author

Edward B. Allen is the author of books for three styles of devotional Bible study. Verse-by-verse books draw devotional points from the Scripture passage in sequence. Historical-people books focus on incidents in the lives of historical people that illustrate biblical principles. Topical books explore relevant Scriptures throughout the Bible. His books also include many personal stories from modern life.

His books are in two series. Books in the *A Slow Walk* series have short meditations in daily-devotional format, such as *A Slow Walk through Psalm 119: 90 Devotional Meditations*. Books in the *Devotional Commentary* series are straight reads with a devotional slant, rather than academic or theological comments, such as *Practical Faith: A Devotional Commentary*.

He has led discussion Bible-study groups in evangelical churches for over 50 years He received a Ph.D. in Computer Science degree at Florida Atlantic University and had a career in software engineering. He has authored or coauthored over 80 professional papers.

www.ingramcontent.com/pod-product-compliance
Lightning Source LLC
Chambersburg PA
CBHW061440040426
42450CB00007B/1140